Cross-stitch

DESIGNS FROM
China

W9-AXF-755

Cross-stitch
DESIGNS FROM
China

CAROL PHILLIPSON

GUILD OF MASTER CRAFTSMAN PUBLICATIONS

First published 2001 by
Guild of Master Craftsman Publications Ltd,
166 High Street, Lewes,
East Sussex, BN7 1XN

Text and illustrations © Carol Phillipson 2001
© in the work GMC Publications Ltd

Photographs by Christine Richardson

ISBN 1 86108 223 1

All rights reserved

The right of Carol Phillipson to be identified as the author
of this work has been asserted in accordance with the
Copyright Designs and Patents Act 1988, Sections 77
and 78.

No part of this publication may be reproduced, stored in
a retrieval system, or transmitted in any form or by any means
without the prior permission of the publisher and copyright
owner.

This book is sold subject to the condition that all designs are
copyright and are not for commercial reproduction without the
written permission of the designer and copyright owner.

The publishers and authors can accept no legal responsibility
for any consequences arising from the application of
information, advice or instructions given in this publication.

British Cataloguing in Publication Data
A catalogue record of this book is available from the British
Library.

Book design by Phil and Traci Morash, Fineline Studios
Typeface: Optima

Cover design by the GMC Studio

Colour separation by Viscan Graphics Pte Ltd (Singapore)

Printed and bound by Kyodo (Singapore) under the supervision
of MRM Graphics, Winslow, Buckinghamshire. UK

Dedication

This book is dedicated to Alan for his whole-hearted support, help and enthusiasm and his never-ending patience. Thank you!

Acknowledgements

Once again, I must thank my daughter Catherine for her help with stitching some of the samples, and many thanks must go to Ann Hebb for her continued enthusiasm and help.

I am grateful and appreciative for the help that I have received from Fabric Flair Ltd (Freephone: 0800 716851) for supplying all of the fabrics

Coats Crafts UK (01325 394237) who supplied all of the threads and yarns

Framecraft Miniatures Ltd. (01212 120551) for many of the accessories

Fireside Reflections (01473 415705) for the wooden clock, footstool, frames

Impress Cards (01986 781422) for supplying a wooden box and cards

I would also like to thank The Commercial Press (Hong Kong) Limited, for permission to use photographs from their publication *Chinese Textile Designs* as source material.

CONTENTS

A note about the 'Thread required' keys

Please note that these keys have been computer-generated and the figures given are the exact amounts of thread used to complete the stitches in the designs. Even the most fastidious needleworker is unlikely to measure their thread to within 0.04cm (¹⁄₁₀in), but the keys may offer useful guidelines.

Introduction

I have always found aspects of the Chinese way of life, before it became a Republic in 1912, mysterious and enchanting. Dragons, phoenixes, pagodas and beautifully embroidered robes were just a small part of the mystical fascination and I have thoroughly enjoyed researching areas involving art and design, in order to create these stitching projects for you.

Textiles, ceramics, art, architecture and sculpture formed the first part of my research, and many of the designs included are adaptations from these. During this initial research, however, I became more and more intrigued by the auspicious characters and the importance of astrology in shaping the Chinese way of life, so I have included snippets of information throughout the book in the hope that you, too, will find them interesting to read.

The first part of the book – a collection of projects – is followed by further designs for you to interpret in your own way. I have not given specific instructions for completing these, but have included materials, charts and helpful tips for each one.

The preparation of this book has given me great pleasure, and I hope it will provide you with many happy hours of stitching.

Materials, Equipment, Stitches

The basic tools to enable you to stitch any (or all) of the designs in this book are simple. I have used fabrics and threads that are readily available, and have included many small designs to use up odd pieces of fabric and remaining threads.

General Accessories

Scissors are important. I have two pairs of needlework scissors: a small, sharp, pointed pair and a large pair. The small ones are only to be used for threads and I have even fastened a piece of wool on the handle to remind the rest of the family. I use the larger ones for cutting canvas, fabric and Vilene. I never use either of these for cutting paper, as this is notorious for blunting even the sharpest scissors.

The most useful item that I have recently acquired is a small pair of round magnets which fit on either side of the fabric that is being stitched and trap the chart, so that it stays in view at the edge of the embroidery frame. They also make a safe place to leave a needle. These are certainly invaluable.

A good light is an investment. Although there are many that are specifically designed for embroiderers, I find a good, well-placed spotlight equally acceptable.

Blunt-ended needles should always be used for counted-thread work, because they don't split and weaken the threads. I find a size 22 or 24 ideal for evenweave and size 18 for canvas-work.

Fabric

I have stated the fabric used for each item in the book. All the fabrics were supplied by Fabric Flair Limited and I have used mainly Aida, Jobelan and canvas. Aida is the easiest to use, but many stitchers, including myself, prefer to work over two threads on Jobelan. A substitute can often be used but, where this may not work, I have given the exact name of the fabric I used. If you are using a different fabric, remember that the higher the thread count, the finer the stitching becomes.

Threads

The majority of the projects in the book are in either stranded cotton or tapestry wool, but I have included some variations, either for the colouring or texture. I find the wide range of threads and colours available a never-ending source of inspiration.

Frames

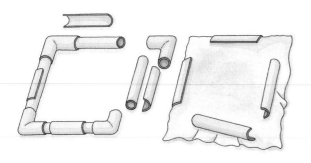

A clip-frame

The use and type of frames is a personal matter. Some stitchers never use one, while others always do. Although sometimes it is tempting not to bother, I always use one because I find the end result more pleasing and it minimizes the need for stretching and adjusting.

Although I have a number of different frames, I really only use three. All my canvas-work and large projects are now done on a clip-frame. These are a recent development and are a collection of light-weight plastic tubes and clips that can be made into a variety of sizes. The fabric is simply laid over the frame and tensioners are placed over to keep it in place. A simple twist adjusts the tension. They really have taken the hard work out of putting fabric on a frame and they don't damage or mark the fabric. For smaller evenweave designs I use a hoop frame, either a wooden seat frame, which leaves both hands free for stitching, or a plastic flexi-hoop for very small items.

Half-cross stitch

Stitches

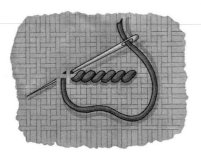

Tent stitch

Although the book is mainly cross stitch I have included half-cross stitch and tent stitch where they are more suitable, to give a variation. Tent stitch gives a better, denser covering than half-cross stitch and is more durable for items that will be subjected to a lot of wear.

First leg of cross stitch

Completion of cross stitch

Adapting Designs

My aim in writing this book is to inspire and interest the stitcher and also to provide a 'library' of Chinese patterns for use whenever they are needed. I have made the stitched pieces up into various decorative objects for the home and have included charts, thread colours, thread counts and details of fabrics used. I have suggested different ideas for use in your own stitched projects, but remember, if you are changing things and experimenting, it is very important to plan before you start stitching, and to make sure the fabric is large enough.

Charted designs can be worked on any fabric with evenly spaced horizontal and vertical threads. These fabrics are known as evenweave and are said to have a 'count', usually expressed in tpi, i.e. the number of threads the fabric has per inch (2.5cm), so, if you are working over every thread, you will work 14 stitches for every inch. Similarly, if you use 28-count fabric but work over two threads (which happens quite often in this book), you are still working 14 stitches in one inch. Stitching a design on a fabric with fewer threads to one inch will enlarge the stitching, but you may then need an extra strand of cotton to cover the canvas or fabric. Always try stitching a small sample and adjust it before starting the main project. Conversely, if the thread count is greater, the work will be smaller, and may need less thread.

One obvious example of this is the last item in Further Designs, the Wooden Box and Card (see page 144). The same chart, when worked on 14-count is suitable for the wooden box-lid, whereas on 22-count it fits the small card aperture. Worked on 7-count it would make a cushion centre.

To calculate the size of a stitched piece, take the pattern size (stitches) and divide it by the number of threads per inch of the fabric. As an example, for a design with 22 squares this will be:

2.5cm (1in) when stitched on 22-count (22 divided by 22)
3cm (1¼in) – 18-count (18 divided by 22)
3.8cm (1½in) – 14-count (14 divided by 22)
5.6cm (2³⁄₁₆in) – 10-count (10 divided by 22)

If you want to make the stitching fit a larger frame, you can add a border or card mount.

Colours are a personal choice. These colours are either the actual Chinese colours, or my choice, but they may not be yours, or they just may not suit your colour scheme. Don't be afraid of changing them. It is usually more successful if you try to keep the darker tones in my design as the darker tones in yours. At the top of the facing page you can see how the pink patchwork cushion flower changes when the colours are altered in the design.

Altering the type of thread, e.g. adding some metallic gold, soft cotton or perle thread, gives a different texture, but you do need to bear in mind the amount of wear the article will receive. For instance, using gold metallic thread in a picture or pot-lid would be fine, but it would soon wear out if used in a rug that was being walked on constantly.

One of my favourite parts of designing is adding the finishing touches. A few beads, a tassel, a twisted cord or a lace edging costs very little, and doesn't take long, but it can make a lot of difference to the completed stitching.

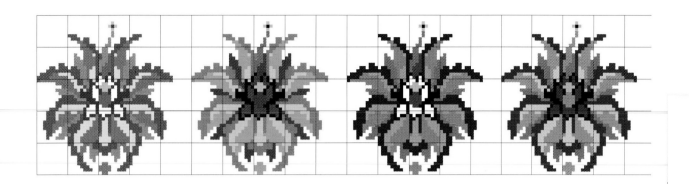

Making a tassel

Take a piece of card slightly longer than the intended length of your tassel. Wrap several layers of thread around the card until it is fairly thick (1). Loop a piece of thread between the card and the wound threads at the top, pull it tight and knot it, then cut the threads from the card at the bottom (2). Smooth the threads down and tightly wind a new length of thread to form a tassel (3). Using a needle, thread the end down so that the secured end becomes part of the tassel. Use the thread at the top to fasten the tassel to the stitching (4).

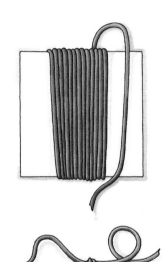

1

2

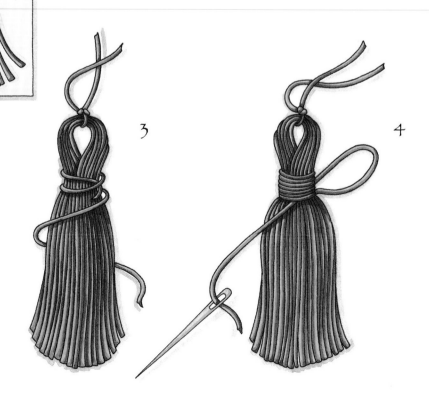

3

4

Making a twisted cord

First decide how long your cord needs to be. Always make it a bit longer than you really want it, because it is easy to trim. I cut the threads three times the required length of the cord, and half as thick as I would like it to be. Fasten a knot at both ends then thread one end over a door handle and thread a pencil through the other (1).

Keeping the thread fairly tight, twist the pencil round and round the same way until it is tightly twisted. Take hold of the twisted thread in the centre and put the two ends together (2). The cord will automatically twist on itself. Remember to keep it taut as you bring the ends together, then it will twist evenly.

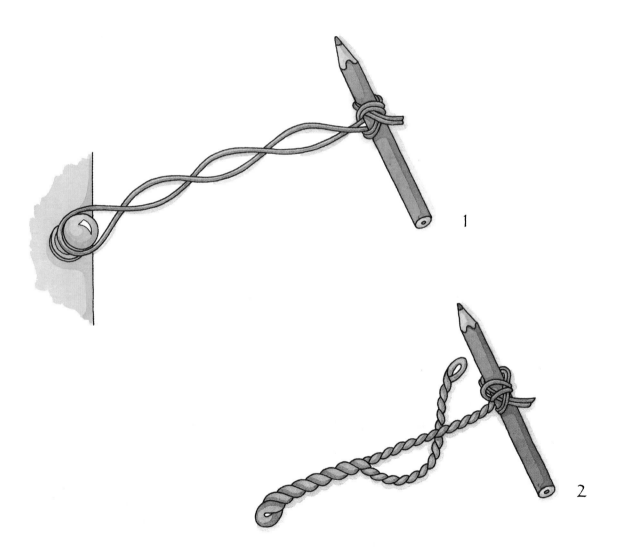

1

2

Helpful Hints

1   Always be well prepared before you start.

2   Don't use very long lengths of thread. Instead of saving time, these become frayed and ragged and need replacing. I find that approximately 45cm (18in) tapestry wool, 30cm (12in) crewel wool, 38cm (15in) stranded cotton and 30cm (12in) of metallic and silk thread give the best results.

3   From time to time let the needle hang free at the back of the work, to allow the thread to untwist.

4   When the work is left on the frame, cover it with a cloth (a tea towel will suffice) to keep it free from dust.

5   If the work is likely to be left for more than a few days, release it from a frame so that it doesn't become marked.

6   While you are stitching, slide the needle along the thread slightly from time to time, to even up the wear on the thread by the needle.

7   Try not to take a break from stitching in the middle of long stretches, as the tension of your stitching may vary slightly when you return to it.

8   Don't carry thread across distances of more than three or four threads at the back, because this causes bulk and can distort the work.

9   Always finish off each end of thread, so that there are no loose ends at the back to become tangled and caught in the stitching.

10   When tapestry work is complete, hold it up to the light to see if any stitches have been missed – if so, fill them in.

Tips for washing/cleaning work

When complete, wool, silk or canvas embroideries should be stretched back into shape; they can then be sprayed with a fabric protector. They must not be washed, but may be dry-cleaned.

Embroidery worked on Aida or Jobelan, using Anchor Stranded Cotton, can be washed using a mild detergent and hot water – as hot as the hand can stand – then rinsed thoroughly. The hot water will set fast the colours. If there is any sign of bleeding from the darker colours, keep rinsing until the water runs clear. The embroidery should be ironed damp, on the wrong side, using a cloth to prevent scorching. A towel or ironing-pad beneath will give the best results. If you are worried about washing your embroidery, it may be dry-cleaned.

THE DESIGNS AND THEIR SOURCES

Auspicious Characters

Numerous symbols are used throughout Chinese design to add messages; in fact, most designs appear to have some symbolic form. These symbols usually wish good fortune and many are concerned with fertility, longevity and wisdom. I have explained some of them for you, partly because they relate to the designs in the book, but also because you may find it interesting to identify the symbols if you see them in Chinese work. It is surprising how frequently they occur.

The auspicious characters fall, more or less, into three categories:

i   Those that are given their meanings simply because they sound similar. The Chinese word for butterfly is 'die' which sounds identical to the word for seventy or eighty years, so butterflies in a design mean a wish for long life, even though butterflies are very short-lived. 'Fu' in Chinese sounds like the word for a bat, and also prosperity, so there are numerous bats in the designs as wishes for prosperity. The lotus flower is called either 'lien' or 'ho'. 'Lien' sounds like the word for united and 'ho' sounds like harmony, so the lotus is a symbol of peace, friendship and a happy union in marriage. The Chinese for a fish is 'yu' which phonetically sounds like the word for abundance and affluence, so a fish in the design signifies wealth. There are many more of these homophones giving meaning to characters.

ii Other symbols take their meanings from the nature of their character or from stories. Pear trees live for a long time – some have been recorded as living for more than 300 years – so a pear in a design means longevity. Pomegranates are a wish for fertility and many sons, because of their numerous yellow seeds. In painting, the pomegranate is frequently shown split open with seeds spilling out of the fruit. A symbol that looks like dried-up fungus often occurs, sometimes held by a stag. This is a 'ligzhi' which, when it is dried, is supposed to last for ever, so it is ground down and used as an elixir of long life. Pines have a similar association with long life because they endure the hard winters.

Manchurian cranes and storks are signs of immortality and longevity and are thought to be the messengers for the God of Longevity called Shou Xing. He is usually shown in art to be a bearded old man, often carrying an old stick in one hand and a peach (a symbol of longevity) in the other. There is a sign which appears in several forms throughout China called the 'shou' (see below) and this also has the meaning of long life. This forms a part of the design on the Aromatic Herb Rope (page 14), the Enamel Bird bookmark (page 97) and the Nail Protector (page 98).

Sometimes more than one auspicious character is included and in this case the blessings combine. For instance, a swastika means ten thousand and the meaning of a bat is happiness and prosperity, so a bat with a swastika in its mouth means ten thousand wishes for happiness.

iii The third source of auspicious symbols is religious and traditional beliefs which include Eight Emblems of Good Fortune, the Eight Precious Things (see overleaf), the Twelve Signs of the Emperor, and the Four Gentlemanly Accomplishments.

The 'shou' sign

Eight Buddhist Emblems of Good Fortune

Eight Emblems of Good Fortune were supposed to have been seen in Buddha's footprints. A wheel or chakra is for the law (a); a conch shell summoned the people to worship (b); a parasol or umbrella means healing (c); a canopy was protection for his people (d); a lotus plant means the purity of the people (e); a vase is to ensure peace throughout the land (f); a pair of fishes is for a time of plenty (g) and an endless knot is for the never-ending mercy of Buddha, and long life (h).

The Twelve Signs of the Emperor are explained in the chapter about Chinese Textiles (see page 37). These occurred frequently.

The Eight Precious Things are a jewel or pearl (a); coins (b); a fangsheng, which is a symbol of victory shown as an open lozenge (c); a book or pair of books (d); a solid lozenge (e); a stone musical chime (f); a pair of rhinoceros horns (g) and an artemisia leaf (h). All of these are intertwined with red ribbons to show that they are like charms and carry a wish for material prosperity.

Every Chinese scholar wanted to excel in music, writing, painting and chess, so each of these has a symbol, too – a lute, books or brushpens, two scrolls and a chess-board. Collectively these are known as the Four Gentlemanly Attributes.

Eight Precious Things

Aromatic Herb Ropes

I have picked out six auspicious characters, used each in a small herb or pot-pourri bag and fastened the bags together to make aromatic ropes. These can be hung up to scent a room, or would make a lovely wedding gift to hand to a bride at the church instead of a horseshoe. You could choose which of the blessings to stitch. The six are a lotus flower, the symbol for peace and a happy marriage, a 'shou' sign for a long life, a bat for prosperity, a peach for longevity, a fish for prosperity and a 'wan' sign for ten thousand times the blessing.

Working the designs

Overcast the edges to prevent fraying. Find the centre of the length and stitch the design so that the centre stitch of the design is on this line, i.e. 9cm (3½in) down from the top. Work the design with two strands of cotton over every thread.

Materials

For each bag:
19-count Easistitch: 18 x 16cm (7 x 6¼in)
Gathered lace: 15cm (6in)
Narrow ribbon: 45cm (18in) of each colour for each bag

To make one rope:
1 brass ring
Thick, white, shiny cord: 45cm (18in)
Small ribbon flower or bow for the end
Polyester filling and scented oil

1 skein of 336, 337, 339, 341, 386, 1, 403, 875, 877, Black and Reflecta 300 will do all six bags

LOTUS

Design size	3.6 x 3.8cm (1⁷⁄₁₀ x 1½in)
Stitch count	27 x 29
Number of strands	2

Thread required

	Anchor Stranded Cotton
	403
	336
	339
	341
	386/336*
	875
	877
	386
	Coats Reflecta 300

*Use 1 strand of each

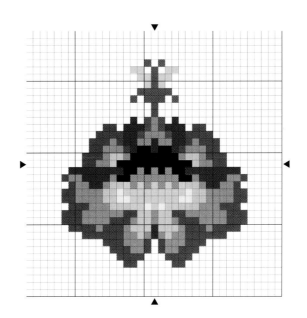

SHOU

Design size	3.6 x 3.8cm (1⁹⁄₁₀ x 1½)
Stitch count	26 x 28
Number of strands	2

Thread required

	Anchor Stranded Cotton
	Coats Reflecta 300

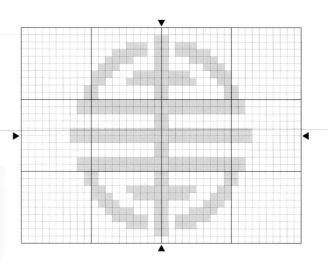

FISH

Design size	4 x 4cm (1⁹⁄₁₀ x 1⁹⁄₁₀in)
Stitch count	30 x 30
Number of strands	2

Thread required

	Anchor Stranded Cotton
	403
	337/336*
	337/339*
	339
	341
	875
	877
	341/Black*

*Use 1 strand of each

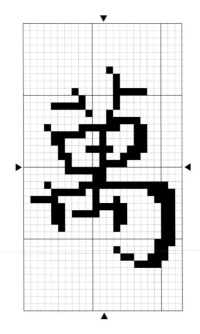

WAN

Design size	2.7 x 3.8cm (1¹⁄₁₀ x 1½in)
Stitch count	21 x 28
Number of strands	2

Thread required

	Anchor Stranded Cotton
	403

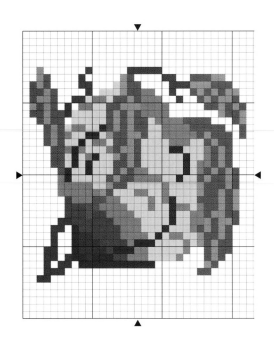

Peach

Design size	4 x 4cm (1⁹⁄₁₀ x 1⁹⁄₁₀in)
Stitch count	31 x 30
Number of strands	2

Thread required

Anchor
Stranded Cotton

	337/336*
	339
	341
	386/336*
	875
	877
	877/Black*
	341/339*

*Use 1 strand of each

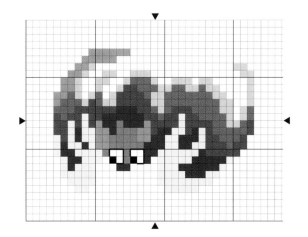

Bat

Design size	3.8 x 2.7cm (1½ x 1¹⁄₁₀in)
Stitch count	29 x 20
Number of strands	2

Thread required

Anchor
Stranded Cotton

	403
	336
	337/336*
	337/339*
	339
	341
	386/336*
	386
	1

*Use 1 strand of each

Making up the designs

Press well on the wrong side using a damp cloth. Make a fold 5cm (2in) above the top of the design and turn the top to the wrong side. Fasten the lace edging on the wrong side, at the top of the fold. With right sides together stitch the 18cm (7in) side seam allowing 1cm (½in) seam allowance. Press the seam open, then stitch across the bottom so that the side seam comes in the centre of the back. Trim the seams, then turn the bag the right way. Repeat this process until you have made the desired number of bags.

Fold the thick cord in half and slip it onto the ring. Wrap the cord round with stranded cotton 7.5cm (3in) from the bottom, then stitch on the flower and unravel the ends of the cord to form a tassel. Fill the bags three quarters full of stuffing, then use the ribbons to seal the tops of the bags. Secure them to the rope, spacing the bags evenly, and finish off with a bow at the front.

Chinese Astrology and Cosmology

The people of China search continuously for harmony and have a strong belief in yin and yang, mystical forces which keep a balanced harmony. The climax of yin is the winter solstice and of yang midsummer. Yin is associated with odd and yang with even, so even years are yang and odd years are yin. The symbol for yin and yang is found throughout Chinese design.

Other forces, compass directions, and the five elements – metal, water, wood, fire and earth – play a part in the creation of the harmony and these affect yin and yang. At favourable times these work together. Wood makes fire, fire-ashes create earth, earth makes metal (as in ore), metal produces water through melting and water makes wood and vegetation grow.

There are many Chinese stories and theories concerning cosmic origins. According to mythology, the origin of Earth was like an egg which split, causing a mythical creature called Phan-Ku (Pan-Gu) to be born. The dark part of the egg became Earth and the light part became the sky. For eighteen thousand years, the earth and sky grew ten feet further apart each day. Phan-Ku grew at exactly the same rate, so his body filled the space and kept them apart. He then died and his head became East, his stomach the centre, his left arm the South, his right arm the North and his feet the West. Rivers and seas came from his tears, his breath was the wind, his eyes became lightning and his voice thunder. Pearls and precious stones were created from his hair, and his teeth and bones became metals and gems.

Another legend says that the first goddess to appear on this new earth was called Nu-Kua (Nu-Wa). She found it too quiet, so she tried to model people out of yellow clay. The first one she made laughed and danced and the world seemed to be a happier place, so she made lots more, but she became bored because it was slow work. She dipped a piece of vine in the mud and let drops of watery mud fall off and these drops became more people. The muddy drops were destined to become the poor and humble people, but the models became the rich and affluent.

In Ancient China it was firmly believed that one's destiny was linked to the moment of birth. Astrology used to be the prerogative of the Emperor and was forbidden to the general public, but it gradually became used by everyone. In fact, until fairly recently, marriage did not take place without the families contacting astrologers to find the chances of success for the joining of the two people. This was determined by a combination of factors: the year animal, the month of birth, the time of birth and the appropriate element, because every year has earth, metal, water, wood or fire associated with it. The astrologer determines whether the particular combination of these is likely to be compatible with those of the partner and his decision is taken very seriously.

I found the development of the Chinese years – which gives the year animal – fascinating, so I designed a wall-hanging representing the years from 2001 to 2012, with their associated astrological animals.

According to legend, Buddha invited all the animal kingdom to celebrate his Enlightenment, but only twelve animals came: a snake, a horse, a monkey, a rooster, a dog, a pig, a rat, a tiger, a hare or rabbit, a sheep or ram, an ox and a dragon. Buddha granted them each a year of rule, so every twelfth year a different animal reigns. The year is determined by Jupiter, known by the Chinese as the Year Star, and therefore does not always start on the same day each year, so I have put the starting date of each year on the stitching. So that you may find your own year animal or that of a friend, I am including a list of the dates from 1950. An unusual birthday card could pertinently be stitched using the birth date and year animal of the recipient.

ANIMALS IN THE CHINESE YEAR

Snakes are not very often used in designs, because they are thought to be mischievous spirits that can be cruel and ruthless. In astrology they are considered to be pleasure-loving and self-reliant, but secretive.

Horses are thought to be noble, friendly, trustworthy, hard-working and generous. Carved horses were put outside tombs to protect the dead from demons and sometimes gods were shown as white horses in the sky.

The sheep, which can also be a goat, is supposed to be gentle, considerate and sympathetic.

Monkeys are 'lovable rogues'. They are conceited and charming, but are resourceful and may be deceptive if it suits their purpose. Legend has it that they were born from an egg fertilized by the wind, and that they gained double immortality.

Roosters are thought to be witty, ambitious and single-minded – especially where their families are concerned – but they can be tactless.

Dogs are honest, intelligent and affectionate and care a lot for their families. There is an interesting folk tale about a dog. There were severe floods throughout the land and when these had subsided a little, the people realised that not only had all their crops been destroyed, but also the seeds, so they hadn't the means to plant another harvest. While they were considering this catastrophe, a dog came out from one of the flooded fields with some long yellow ears of what looked like a crop caught on its tail. The people planted these when the floods cleared and rice grew, so they were able to grow food again.

Pigs are loyal, caring, reliable and sociable and they nurture their families.

The rat, my own year symbol, is supposed to be hard-working, thrifty and very ambitious. I am not prepared to say how true this is!

The ox is even more hard-working than the rat, but has a stubborn tendency. In mythology the ox was originally a star in the sky. Man on Earth was struggling to find enough food to eat and often only ate two or three times a week. This upset the Emperor of Heaven so he sent the ox from the star to tell the people that if they worked very hard, the Emperor would help them and make sure that they had a good meal at least every third day. The ox jumbled up the message and told them that the Emperor would help them to eat three times a day. There wasn't any way the men could do enough ploughing to enable this to happen, so the Emperor sent the ox permanently back down to earth to help.

Tigers are the 'kings' of the animals in China. People with the tiger as their birth animal are supposed to be born lucky, but they need to be, because they are often reckless and daring. Tigers are often used to decorate children's garments in China, to protect them from danger.

The hare or rabbit is thought to be lucky and is known for its generosity and artistic talents, while dragon year people are energetic, strong-willed and very protective of their own interests.

These twelve animals are also concerned with feng shui, which is mentioned again in the section on Chinese Buildings (see page 71).

Chinese Year
Astrological Wall-hanging

Working the design

Overcast the edges of the Jobelan to prevent fraying then, starting in the centre, stitch the design using two strands of cotton and working over two threads.

Making up the design

Press the stitching on the wrong side using a damp cloth. Centre the large piece of Vilene on the back of the stitching and iron in place. Trim the edges to 2.5cm (1in) outside the edge of the Vilene. Turn the edges to the back and secure by ironing the strips of Vilene over the edges.

Make four hanging loops. Turn under 2cm (¾in) on the long sides of the Jobelan, then secure with the Vilene strips. Do the same with the top and bottom of the Jobelan. Now fold and tack the loops evenly across the top of the wall-hanging, placing those on the edge 2cm (¾in) from the ends. The loops should be 4cm (1‰in) high. Machine a line of plain stitching (or back stitching, if by hand) 1cm (½in) from the outside edge to both form an edge to the hanging and also secure the hanging loops. Slot the bamboo through and tie on the hanging cord.

Materials
Jobelan 28-count: 86.5 x 30cm (34 x 12in)
Iron-on Vilene:
    1 piece 80 x 26cm (31½in x 10¼in)
    2 pieces 79 x 5cm (31 x 2in)
    2 pieces 25.5 x 5cm (10 x 2in)
For hanging loops:
    4 pieces Jobelan 10 x 18cm (4 x 7in)
    4 pieces Vilene 6.5 x 10cm (2½in x 4in)
    8 pieces Vilene 2.5 x 10cm (1 x 4in)
Bamboo cane 81.5cm (32in)
Hanging cord: 1m (39in)
Threads as listed

Design size	79.3 x 21.8cm (31⅖₀ x 8⅗₀in)
Stitch count	437 x 120
Number of strands	2

Thread required

	Anchor Stranded Cotton	Amount
	403	1562.4cm (615⅒in)
	882	1735.5cm (683⅗₀in)
	232	59.3cm (23⅜₀in)
	1098	296.4cm (116⅞₀in)
	232/1080**	894.6cm (352⅗₀in)
	266	245.4cm (96⅝₀in)
	403*	170.8cm (67⅜₀in)
	1098*	0.2cm (⅒in)

*Back stitch **Use 1 strand of each

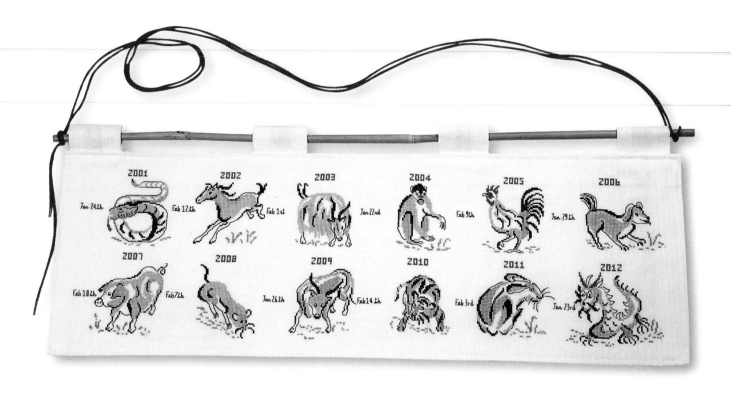

A black and white version of this chart, which can be enlarged on a photocopier for easier working, can be found on pages 148 and 149

The Chinese Calendar from 1950 to 2000   (each is the starting date)

1950	Feb 17	Tiger	1967	Feb 9	Sheep	1984	Feb 2	Rat
1951	Feb 6	Hare	1968	Jan 30	Monkey	1985	Feb 20	Ox
1952	Jan 27	Dragon	1969	Feb 17	Rooster	1986	Feb 9	Tiger
1953	Feb 14	Snake	1970	Feb 6	Dog	1987	Jan 29	Hare
1954	Feb 3	Horse	1971	Jan 27	Pig	1988	Feb 17	Dragon
1955	Jan 24	Sheep	1972	Feb 15	Rat	1989	Feb 6	Snake
1956	Feb 12	Monkey	1973	Feb 3	Ox	1990	Jan 27	Horse
1957	Jan 31	Rooster	1974	Jan 23	Tiger	1991	Feb 15	Ram
1958	Feb 18	Dog	1975	Feb 11	Hare	1992	Feb 4	Monkey
1959	Feb 8	Pig	1976	Jan 31	Dragon	1993	Jan 23	Rooster
1960	Jan 28	Rat	1977	Feb 18	Snake	1994	Feb 10	Dog
1961	Feb 15	Ox	1978	Feb 7	Horse	1995	Jan 31	Pig
1962	Feb 6t	Tiger	1979	Jan 28	Ram	1996	Feb 19	Rat
1963	Jan 25	Hare	1980	Feb 16	Monkey	1997	Feb 7	Ox
1964	Feb 13	Dragon	1981	Feb 5	Rooster	1998	Jan 28	Tiger
1965	Feb 2	Snake	1982	Jan 25	Dog	1999	Feb 16	Hare
1966	Jan 21	Horse	1983	Feb 13	Pig	2000	Feb 5	Dragon

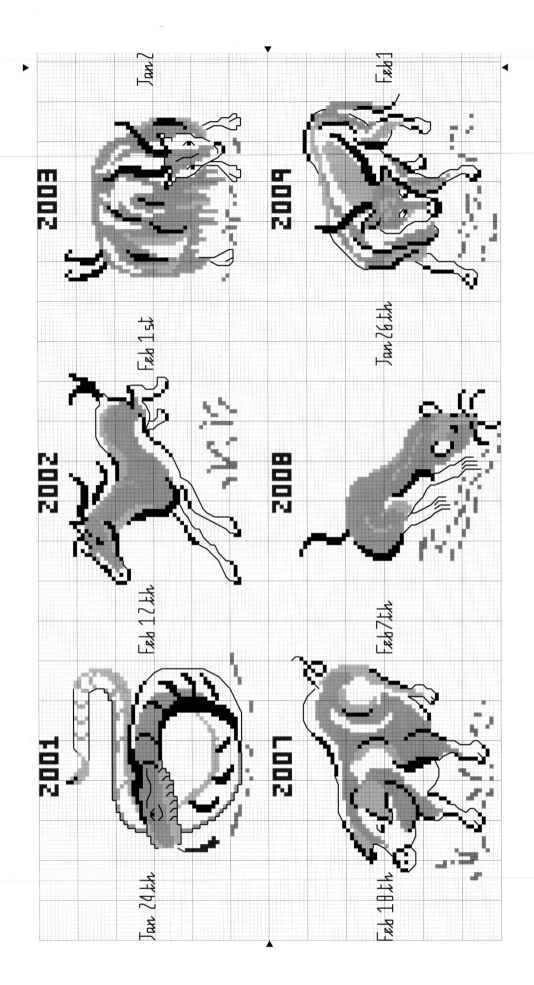

2003   Jan 2

2004   Feb 1

2002   Feb 1st   Jan 26th

2008   Feb 7th

2001   Feb 12th   Jan 24th

2007   Feb 18th

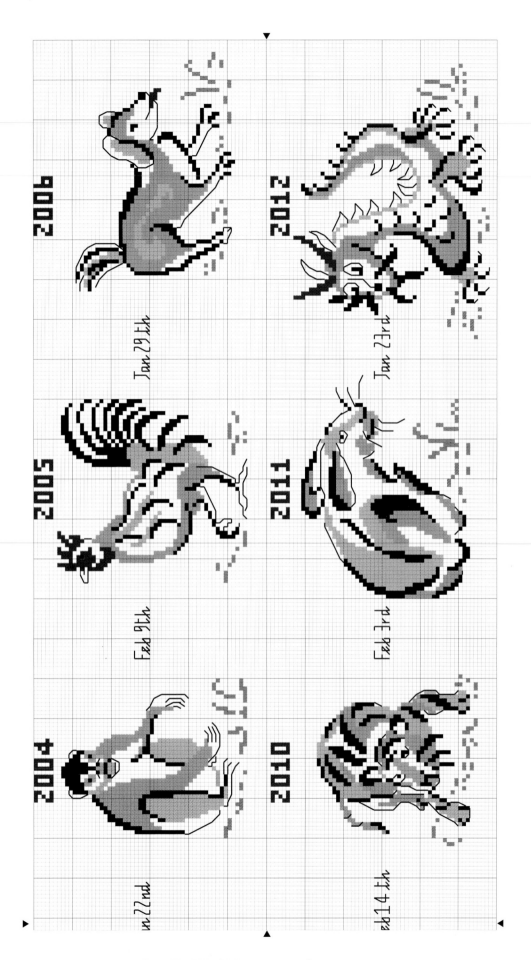

2006

Jan 29th

2005

Feb 9th

2004

un 22nd

2012

Jan 23rd

2011

Feb 3rd

2010

eb 14th

Chinese Ceramics

C hina is renowned for its fine porcelain and enamelling and a number of the stitched pieces in this book were inspired by Chinese porcelain, stoneware and enamelled objects which were used as serving, storage, decorative and funereal vessels. I have included at least one of each and, where it is appropriate, I have given the source of the design and a brief information section. Many of the objects that I looked at were decorated in *cloisonné*

enamelling, a technique in which fine wires are attached to a metal base and then enamel colouring is applied. The object is fired in a kiln, causing the enamel to melt, but the colour is contained within the wire borders. The article is polished smooth and the wire lines are gilded, so giving raised gold edges to the colours. The 'Enamel Bird' bookmark in Further Designs is an example of this (see page 97).

Two Shaped Ginger-jar Cushions

DRAGON CUSHION

These designs were inspired by a variety of blue and white porcelain vases and I thought the ginger jar shape was particularly suitable for an interesting cushion. Jars of this shape were used throughout China to store spices and pickles.

The dramatic dragon design here was inspired by several large porcelain vases and it is shown among the clouds, which are so much a feature of Chinese dragon designs.

Working the design

Stitch the design using a single strand of wool and tent stitch in the centre of the canvas. When it is complete, work one row of cross stitch in 8638 all the way round the outside to give a firm edge.

Making up the design

Block the stitching if necessary, then cut out the design, leaving 2cm (¾in) seam allowance. Cut a piece of backing fabric the same size (including the seam allowance).

Put right sides together and stitch carefully round the shape, but leave 12.7cm (5in) gap in the centre-bottom to allow for turning through. Trim the turnings to two canvas threads (apart from the edges of the opening), then turn the right way. Fill with stuffing, using a chunky knitting needle to guide and push the stuffing and ensure that all the corners are filled.

Slip stitch over the opening with 8638, to close it up. Make a twisted cord, approximately 120cm (4ft), using leftover colours, or buy some cord and fasten it all the way round the sides and top. Fasten chunky tassels to each corner.

Materials

12-count canvas 38 x 53cm (15 x 21in)
Backing fabric 35.5 x 51cm (14 x 20in)
Stuffing
2 Tassels and 120cm (47in) thick cord
Threads
Anchor Tapestry Wool
For the background: three hanks of 8004
For the design: seven skeins of 8638; three of 8636; two of 8634; five of 8632; and one of 8630

Design size	32.4 x 45cm (12⅘ x 18in)
Stitch count	153 x 216
Number of strands	1 x Wool

Thread colours required for both designs

Anchor
Tapestry Wool

	8638
	8636
	8634
	8632
	8630
	8628
	8624
	8004

A black and white version of this chart, which can be enlarged on a photocopier for easier working, can be found on page 150

MANDARIN DUCK CUSHION

The inspiration for this design came from a Meiping porcelain vase from the Ming dynasty (1368–1644). It shows a mandarin duck among lotus plants.

Working the design

Use a single strand of wool to tent stitch the design in the centre of the canvas. Once the design is complete, work one row of cross stitch in 8638 all the way round the outside, to give a firm edge.

Making up the design

Follow instructions for making up the Dragon Cushion (see page 24).

Materials
12-count canvas 38 x 53cm (15 x 21in)
Backing fabric 35.5 x 51cm (14 x 20in)
Stuffing
Threads:
Anchor Tapestry Wool
For the background: three hanks of 8004
For the design: seven skeins of 8638; two of 8636; three of 8634; four of 8632; three of 8630; three of 8628 and four of 8624

Design size	32.4 x 45cm (12⁹⁄₁₀ x 18in)
Stitch count	153 x 216
Number of strands	1 x Wool

A black and white version of this chart, which can be enlarged on a photocopier for easier working, can be found on page 151

Metallic Flower Bell-pull

For this I used flowers from different ceramic vases and pots, then linked them together using some of the scroll designs found throughout Chinese art. To give it more vibrancy, I added touches of metallic gold and red. This makes a stunning bell-pull and it is very pleasant to stitch, because it divides easily into small areas and each area can be completed fairly quickly. I used natural wood bell-pull ends because I didn't want to detract from the stitching, but you could easily stain them in a colour to match the flowers.

Materials

28-count Jobelan 89 x 20cm (35 x 8in)
Iron on Vilene:
- one piece 84 x 14cm (33 1/2 x 5 1/2in)
- two pieces 5 x 84cm (2 x 33 1/2in)
- two pieces 5 x 14cm (2 x 5 1/2in)

15cm (6in) Wooden bell-pull ends (these come in longer lengths, but are simple to cut down)
Threads as listed

Design size	16.3 x 71.5cm (6 4/10 x 28 1/10in)
Stitch count	90 x 394
Number of strands	2

Working the design

Overcast the edges to prevent fraying, then stitch the design in the centre of the fabric using two strands of stranded cotton over two threads, and three strands of metallic lamé.

Making up the design

Press well on the wrong side, using a damp cloth. Centre the large piece of Vilene on the back of the stitching, then iron it in place, making sure that the threads are straight. Trim the excess fabric from the long side edges to 2.5cm (1in), then turn these in and secure using the two long pieces of Vilene. Trim the top to 7.5cm (3in), then turn down and secure in the same way using one of the shorter strips; remember to leave a slot for the bell-pull rod to go through. Trim the bottom to 7.5cm (3in) then turn down and secure, again leaving a slot. Fasten in the bell-pull ends, then use a 30cm (12in) length of the metallic thread as a hanger, knotting it at the ends of the rod.

Thread required

Anchor Stranded Cotton	Amount
214	656.2cm (258 3/10in)
877	614.9cm (242 1/10in)
878	357.0cm (140 6/10in)
1024/White**	170.4cm (67 1/10in)
39	157.0cm (61 8/10in)
59	283.9cm (111 8/10in)
314	122.7cm (48 3/10in)
316	208.4cm (82in)
326	311.6cm (122 7/10in)
400/White**	23.2cm (9 1/10in)
400	107.0cm (42 1/10in)
134	497.8cm (196in)
134/White**	295.9cm (116 1/2in)
Gold Lamé 303†	104.8cm (266 3/10in)
Red Lamé 318†	160.2cm (63 1/10in)
1	417.2cm (164 3/10in)
59/White**	185.2cm (72 9/10in)
39/White**	79.2cm (31 2/10in)
316/White**	50.5cm (19 9/10in)
Gold Lamé*††	1cm (4/10in)
59*	18.1cm (7 1/10in)
Red Lamé 318*	0.2cm (1/10in)
400*	9.3cm (3 7/10in)

*Back stitch ** Use 1 strand of each †Use 3 strands
††Use 4 strands

Lower half

A black and white version of this chart, which can be enlarged on a photocopier for easier working, can be found on pages 152–3

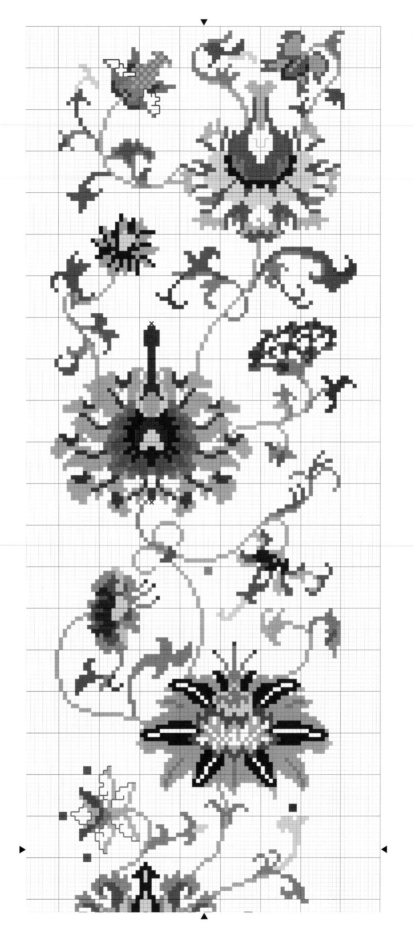

Pair of Flowery Towel Borders

These colourful borders were inspired by painted china bowls. I worked them on 28-count fabric and stitched them onto plain towels. Cream adds a touch of luxury without detracting from the colours in the design. They have small amounts of metallic thread in them, but this could easily be replaced by Anchor Stranded Cotton 298.

Materials

For each towel you will need;

28-count Jobelan 53 x 12.7cm (21 x 5in)

(As this is worked over two threads, 14-count could be substituted)

Towel of your choice. If it is a large towel the fabric length may need to be extended. Allow 2.5cm (1in) extra at each side of the towel.

Working the design

Overcast the edges to prevent fraying, then work the design in the centre of the fabric.

Making up the design

Press the embroidery on the wrong side, using a damp cloth. Turn in the side and end seams then attach to the towel.

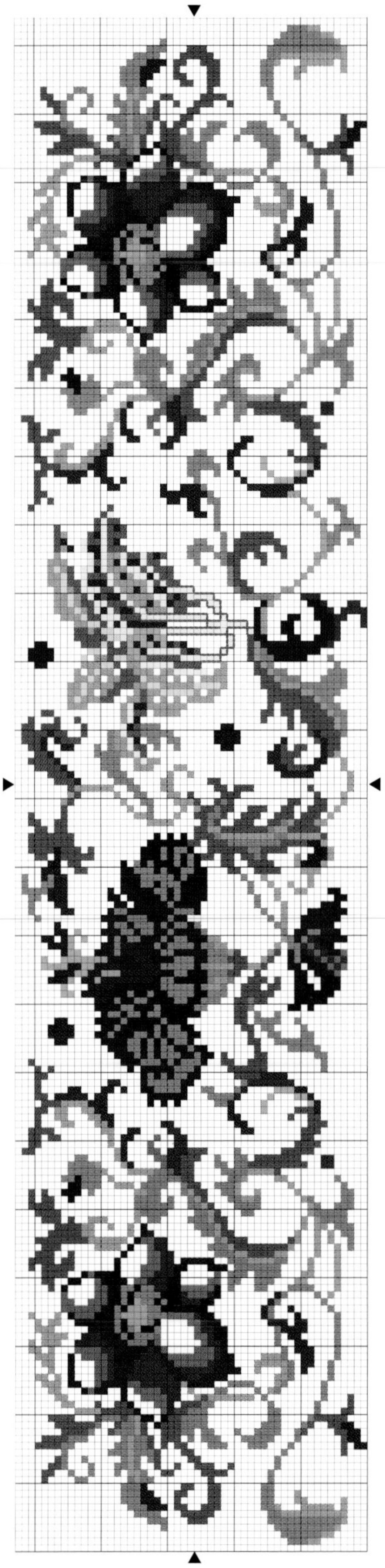

Thread required

	Anchor Stranded Cotton	Amount
	1	87.1cm (34$\frac{3}{10}$in)
	1066	372.3cm (146$\frac{6}{10}$in)
	1064	425.1cm (167$\frac{4}{10}$in)
	1060	263.5cm (103$\frac{7}{10}$in)
	46	150.5cm (59$\frac{2}{10}$in)
	335	113cm (44$\frac{1}{2}$in)
	316	106.5cm (41$\frac{9}{10}$in)
	1036	220.4cm (86$\frac{8}{10}$in)
	1033	136.1cm (53$\frac{6}{10}$in)
	59	84.7cm (33$\frac{4}{10}$in)
	76	73.6cm (29in)
	74	81cm (31$\frac{9}{10}$in)
	386	60.2cm (23$\frac{7}{10}$in)
	1014	101.9cm (40$\frac{1}{10}$in)
	338	50.9cm (20$\frac{1}{10}$in)
	Gold lamé 303†	41.2cm (16$\frac{2}{10}$in)
	74/White**	18.1cm (7$\frac{1}{10}$in)
	1034*	12.3cm (4$\frac{9}{10}$in)

*Back stitch **Use 1 strand of each †Use 4 strands

Design size	40.3 x 9.4cm (15.9 x 3.7in)
Stitch count	222 x 52
Number of strands	2

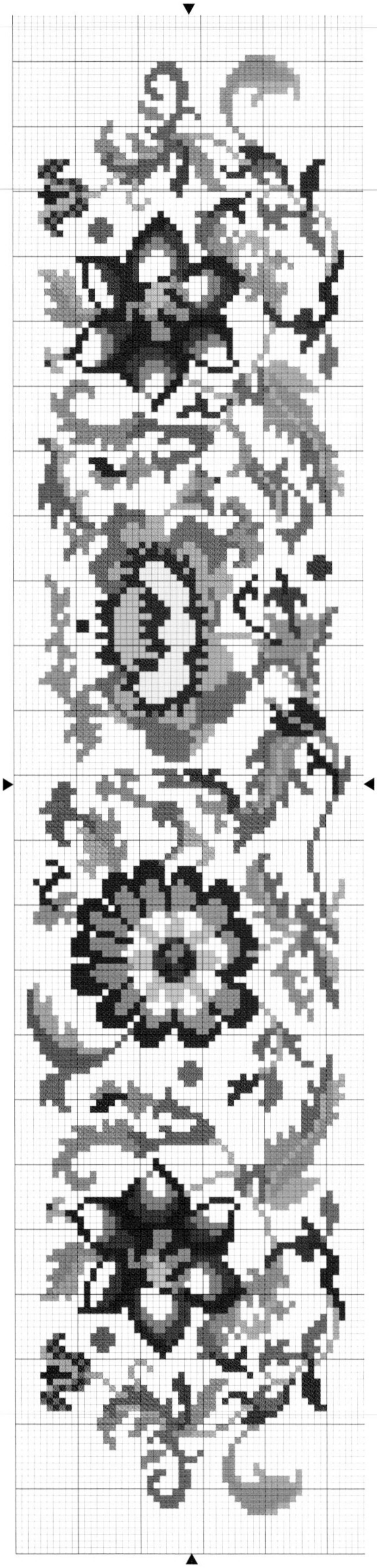

Thread required

	Anchor Stranded Cotton	Amount
	1	107.9cm (42½in)
	1066	395.5cm (155 7/10in)
	1064	426.5cm (167 9/10in)
	1060	271.4cm (106 8/10in)
	46	194.5cm (76 6/10in)
	335	124.1cm (48 9/10in)
	316	83.8cm (33in)
	1036	211.6cm (83 3/10in)
	1033	146.3cm (57 6/10in)
	59	129.2cm (50 9/10in)
	76	155.1cm (61 1/10in)
	74	99.6cm (39 2/10in)
	386	50.9cm (20 1/10in)
	1014	63.0cm (24 8/10in)
	338	35.2cm (13 9/10in)
	Gold lamé 303†	75.5cm (29 7/10in)

†Use 4 strands

Design size	40.8 x 9.4cm (16 1/10 x 3 7/10in)
Stitch count	225 x 52
Number of strands	2

Beaded Band Sampler

A collection of borders is invaluable, so I decided to put together several borders as an attractive band sampler. Each of these could be used separately and extended easily to a required length. I took all of these from patterns on ceramic vases and plates, but changed the colouring to suit the overall design. The colours could easily be adapted to match individual requirements.

Working the design

Overcast the edges to prevent fraying, then work the design in cross stitch, in the centre of the fabric, using two strands of cotton over two threads. Add the beads using one strand of 386.

Making up the design

Place on a thick towel and press on the wrong side, using a damp cloth. Stretch and frame as you wish.

Design size	21 x 26.4cm (8³/₁₀ x 10³/₁₀in)
Stitch count	132 x 166
Number of strands	2

Thread required

	Anchor Stranded Cotton	Amount
	119	314.8cm (123³/₁₀in)
	118	234.2cm (92²/₁₀in)
	108	369.9cm (145⁶/₁₀in)
	188	694.9cm (273³/₁₀in)
	186	387.3cm (152⁵/₁₀in)
	185	340.3cm (134in)
	386	389.8cm (153½in)
	Mill Hill 60168*	
	Mill Hill 00525*	
	Mill Hill 00123*	

*Beads

Materials

32-count evenweave fabric 40.5 x 28cm (16 x 11in) (this is worked over two threads, so 16-count can be substituted)

Mill Hill Beads: 60168 x 182
　　　　　　　　 00525 x 71
　　　　　　　　 00123 x 127

Beading needle

Threads as listed

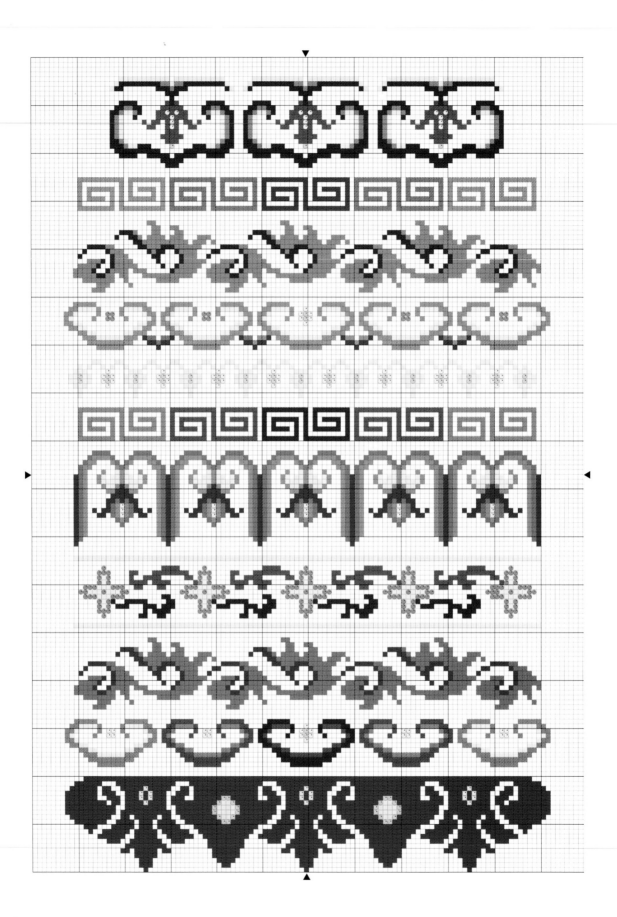

Chinese Textiles

I find textiles from China a never-ending source of inspiration, not only because they are extremely decorative and attractive but also because there are so many varied examples.

China is known as the Silk Country. Silk was first developed in China from silkworms and was used for clothes, furnishings and as a surface for painting on. It was taken out of China during the Han dynasty (206BC–AD220) and was in demand because it was far superior to anything similar. Merchants following caravan routes carried the woven, embroidered or printed silk to the Middle East, the Mediterranean and into parts of Europe. These well-used trails became known as the Silk Route or Silk Road.

The embroidery on some of the fabrics, especially those from the Imperial Palace, is exquisite, with fine detail and colour. During the Ch'ing dynasty (1644–1911) yellow was the prerogative of the Emperor.

Dragon Robes are fascinating and beautifully embroidered, and can be found in many Chinese collections. They were mainly worn during the Qing dynasty (1644–1912) and only the Emperor and selected members of his household were allowed to wear them. The robes had recognizable features, such as thin diagonal stripes along the edges to represent the dragon's home among waves and clouds. In among the clouds twelve symbols, which signified sovereignty, adorned the Emperor's garments: a red disk for the sun, a light blue circle containing a hare for the moon; three golden disks for a constellation of stars; mountains for a rock; dragons; a pheasant to represent the natural world; a 'fu' symbol for good and evil; an axe to show the Imperial power, and the four elements, metal, water, wood and fire. Many other auspicious characters found on textiles are explained throughout the text and several more designs from textiles are in Further Designs (see pages 92–144).

Butterfly Footstool

Materials

Circular pine footstool, with a working area of 30cm (12in) (I used one from Fireside Reflections)

14-count canvas 38cm (15in) square

Frame for working: optional, but I recommend using a square or rectangular frame so that the work does not go out of shape.

Threads: Anchor Tapisserie wools as listed

Thread required

	Anchor Tapisserie wool	Amount
	9800	213.9cm (84⅗in)
	8102	611.2cm (240⅝in)
	8120	765.4cm (301⅜in)
	8606	105.6cm (41⅗in)
	8610	47.2cm (18⅗in)
	9562	351.5cm (138⅜in)
	8052	791.8cm (311⅘in)
	8000 (White)	839.1cm (330⅜in)
	8898	384.8cm (151½in)
	8902	211.2cm (83⅒in)
	8692	1330.8cm (523⅗in)
	8690	890.5cm (350⅗in)
	8688	650.1cm (256in)
	8596	20.8cm (8⅕in)
	8686	339.0cm (133½in)
	8586	276.4cm (108⅘in)
	8590	295.9cm (116½in)
	8596	183.4cm (72⅖in)
	8584	163.9cm (64½in)
	8530	134.7cm (53⅒in)
	8528	197.3cm (77⅗in)
	8526	41.7cm (16⅖in)
	8522	273.7cm (107⅘in)

I used this design, which was based on a cushion-cover design from the Qing dynasty (1644–1912), because I thought the shape of the butterfly matched the round stool-top. The butterfly is a blessing for long life and happiness and the peonies stand for wealth and honour. The colours of the design on the black background are set off by the pine footstool. I have given details for the design itself, but not for the background, because this can be extended or reduced to fit any stool. It is useful to buy black wool for the background in hanks rather than skeins.

Working the design

Stitch the design in the centre of the canvas using tent stitch with one strand of wool.

A black and white version of this chart, which can be enlarged on a photocopier for easier working, can be found on page 154

Making up the design

Stretch the stitched work back into shape if necessary, then stretch it evenly over the stool insert and staple it on the underside. Once it is firmly attached, trim the excess canvas and insert into the stool.

Design size	25 x 25cm (9⁹⁄₁₀ x 9⁹⁄₁₀in)
Stitch count	138 x 138
Number of strands	1 x wool

Peony Clock-face

When I first saw this mahogany clock I had just been studying tree peonies on some old Chinese textiles and a fan tapestry from the Yuan dynasty, and I could imagine how well they would look on the clock face. As the design needed detail, I worked on 22-count evenweave fabric and, in order to make it delicate, I used only half-cross stitch. I was very pleased with the finished article. It would be easy to change the colouring to match a room setting by keeping the greens and the white, but replacing the four shades of browny pink.

Working the design

Overcast the edges to prevent fraying, then stitch the design in half-cross stitch, using two strands and working over each thread.

Making up the design

Press well on the wrong side using a damp cloth. Iron the circle of Vilene onto the back of the stitching, making sure that the design is in the centre. Follow the manufacturer's instructions for making up.

Thread required

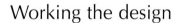

	Anchor Stranded Cotton	Amount
	842	81cm (31 9/10in)
	843	241.6cm (95 1/10in)
	846	197.7cm (77 8/10in)
	893	61.6cm (24 2/10in)
	895	114.6cm (45 1/10in)
	896	127cm (50in)
	897	97.5cm (38 4/10in)
	White/893*	79.3cm (31 2/10in)
	1	130.2cm (51 3/10in)
	905	23cm (9in)

*Use 1 strand of each

Materials

22-count evenweave fabric 23cm (9in) square

Clock: the one shown is a circular mahogany clock with a gold chapter ring from Fireside Reflections. It has a working area of 12.7cm (5in)

Iron-on Vilene: 20cm (8in) circle

Threads as listed

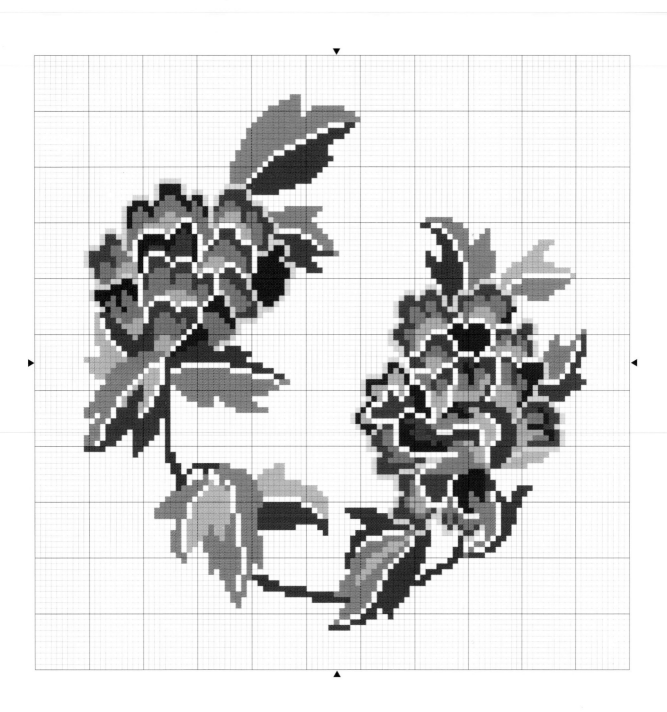

Design size	10.7 x 11.1cm (4²⁄₁₀ x 4⁴⁄₁₀in)
Stitch count	93 x 96
Number of strands	2

Three Butterfly Cushion Centres

There are twelve Chinese butterfly designs, which could all be used together as a set. I made up these three as cushion centres, using butterfly fabric for the backing and embellishing each one with a small amount of gold metallic lamé.

The other butterfly designs are in Further Designs: three are appliquéd onto a towel (page 115), five decorate a top-cloth (page 117) and one is on a small pot-pourri cushion (page 120). All the butterfly designs were adapted from chair covers of a 'hundred butterflies' which were used at the Imperial Palace during the Qing dynasty (1644–1912).

Working each design

Overcast the edges to prevent fraying, then work the design in the centre using two strands and working in cross-stitch over two threads.

Making up each design

Press the embroidery on the wrong side, using a damp cloth. Stitch it in the centre of the front piece of cotton, then tack and stitch the ribbon round the outside to cover the edges. Insert the optional zip into the backing at this stage. With right sides facing stitch together to form a 36cm (14in) square. If you have inserted a zip, make sure that it is partly open to allow the work to be turned through, otherwise leave a 8cm (3in) gap. Trim excess seam allowance. Turn the work through and insert the cushion pad. Either zip up the back, or slip stitch the opening closed.

Design size	10.5 x 9.2cm (4.1 x 3.6in)
Stitch count	58 x 51
Number of strands	2

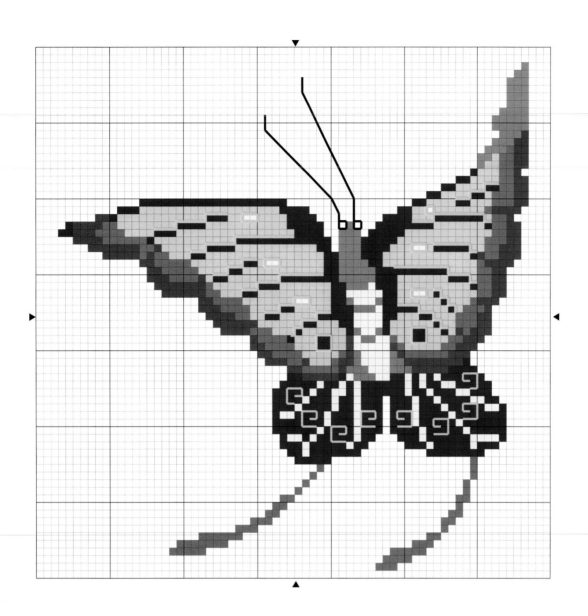

Materials

For each cushion you will need;

28-count Jobelan 18cm (7in) square

Cotton fabric: 2 x 16in squares, one for the front and one for the backing. If you wish to put in a zip, cut the backing 5cm (2in) longer

Ribbon, 63 x 1cm wide (25 x ½in)

Zip, 30cm (12in) (optional)

Cushion pad, 40.5cm (16in)

Threads as listed

Thread required

	Anchor Stranded Cotton	Amount
	386	52.3cm (20⁹⁄₁₀in)
	175	19cm (7½in)
	175/White**	195.9cm (77¹⁄₁₀in)
	176	90.3cm (35½in)
	177	80.1cm (31½in)
	178	225cm (88⁹⁄₁₀in)
	178/386	24.5cm (9⁷⁄₁₀in)
	403* (Eyes/antennae)	5.7cm (2²⁄₁₀in)
	Gold lamé 303*† (Wings)	27.3cm (10⁹⁄₁₀in)

*Back stitch   **Use 1 strand of each   †Use 4 strands

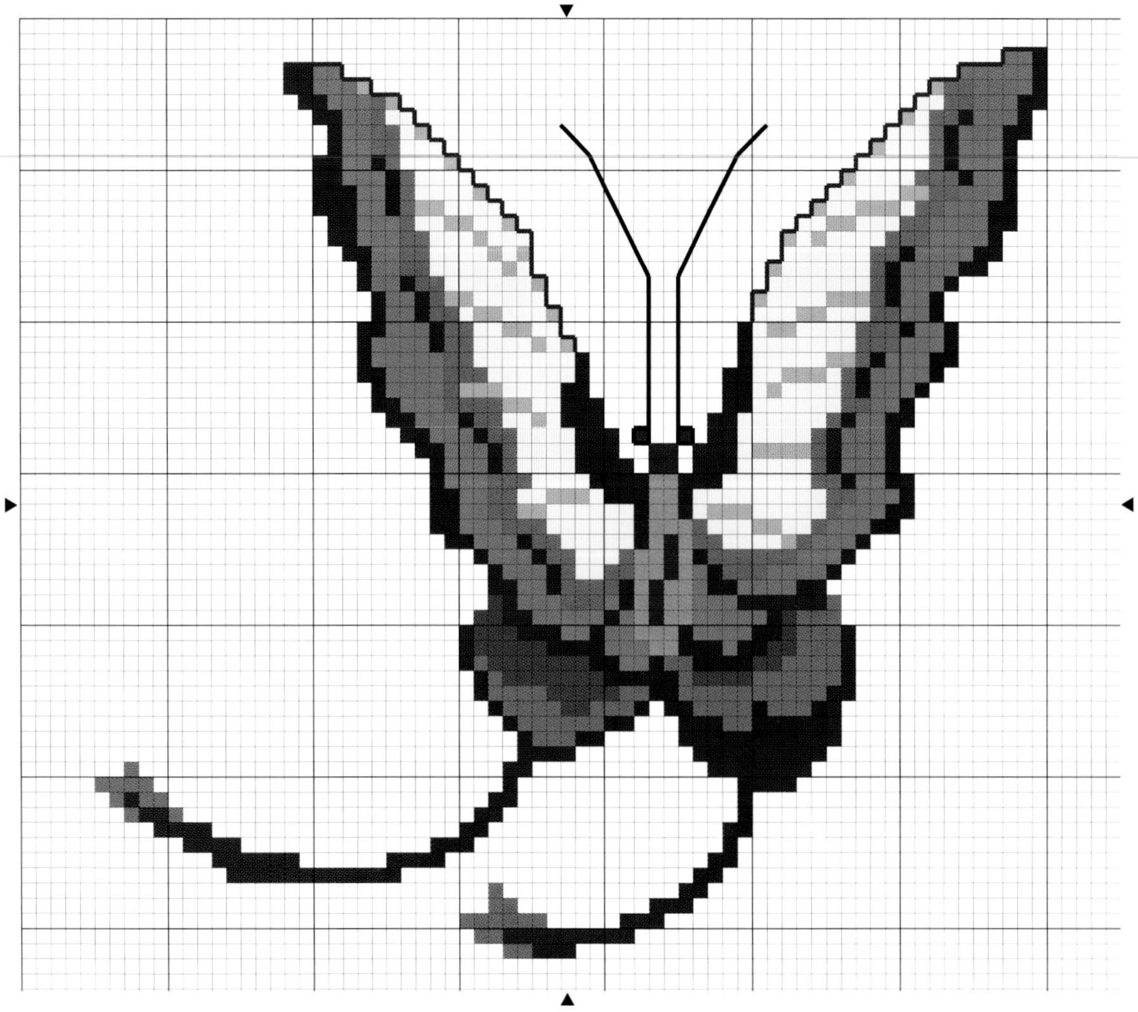

Thread required

	Anchor Stranded Cotton	Amount
	899	14.4cm (5 7/10in)
	386	126cm (49 6/10in)
	Gold lamé 303†	34.3cm (13 1/2in)
	1084	6.9cm (2 7/10in)
	98	100.9cm (39 7/10in)
	101	67.1cm (26 4/10in)
	78	19.4cm (7 7/10in)
	1028	109.7cm (43 2/10in)
	76	110.7cm (43 6/10in)
	403*	6.3cm (2 1/2in)
	101*	9.3cm (3 7/10in)

*Back stitch †Use 4 strands

Design size	12.2 x 11.8cm (4 8/10 x 4 6/10in)
Stitch count	67 x 64
Number of strands	2

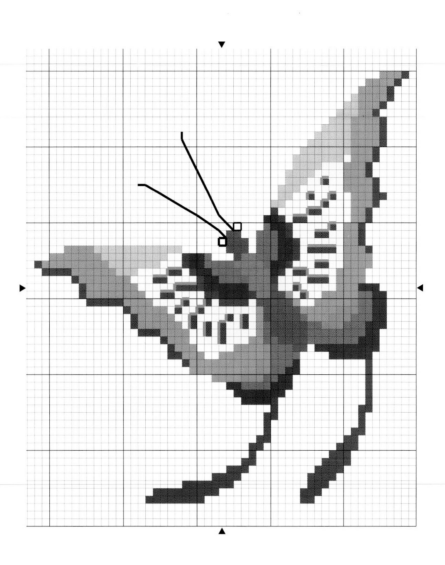

Thread required

	Anchor Stranded Cotton	Amount
	Gold Lamé 303†	8.8cm (3½in)
	217	40.3cm (15‰in)
	215	36.6cm (14‰in)
	944	93.5cm (36‰in)
	943	107.9cm (42½in)
	926	83.4cm (32‰in)
	943/White**	40.3cm (15‰in)
	944/White**	19.9cm (7‰in)
	944/943**	8.3cm (3‰in)
	403*	4.5cm (1‰in)
	Gold Lamé thread*†	7.5cm (3in)

*Back stitch   **Use1 strand of each   †Use 4 strands

Design size	11.8 x 10.9cm (4‰ x 4‰in)
Stitch count	65 x 60
Number of strands	2

Pair of Miniature Chinese Rugs

Because of the heat and humidity, carpets in China were not necessarily used on floors as they are here. Many were used to throw over tables, to put on stone benches to make them more comfortable, or as saddle rugs. There were even some special, very cleverly designed rugs which wrapped around pillars in palaces and temples.

More luxurious carpets were woven from silk, but these were very expensive and not as hard-wearing as those made from the wool of sheep and camels.

In keeping with most Chinese design, auspicious characters were used throughout the carpets, the most common being symbolic flowers, emblems of good fortune and longevity and characters concerned with Buddhism.

I have stitched the two rugs in this section in stranded cotton, rather than wool, to give an impression of the silky sheen, although they don't have quite the feel of silk.

MINIATURE CHINESE RUG 1

This design has been adapted from a large eighteenth-century carpet which had a repetitive design, so I have put together the symbols from this, which occur frequently throughout Chinese design, to make a miniature rug. The outside border has two variations on the 'shou' character which symbolizes longevity, while the inside symbol of a butterfly symbolizes harmony.

Working the design

Stitch the design in the centre of the canvas using tent stitch with three threads.

Materials

22-count canvas, 20 x 16cm (8 x 6¼in)

Threads as listed

Making up the design

Stretch the design back into shape if necessary, then trim the side edges to five threads and turn them to the back, stitching them by hand using a slip stitch or herringbone stitch. Turn the two ends back and stitch in the same way, but leave one thread of the canvas not turned behind. This will have the fringed knots worked on it.

Fringed knots

Thread a needle with six strands of Anchor 386.

1. Pass the needle from the front to the back, through the first empty hole on the left, and leave approximately 4cm (1⁹⁄₁₀in) of thread hanging. Bring the threaded needle back to the front through the third hole (i.e. leave one empty hole) then, leaving an end of approximately 4cm (1⁹⁄₁₀in) hanging, cut off the needle. Keep the needle threaded ready for the next knot.
2. Tuck both thread ends down through the loop.
3. Tighten the loop to form a knot.
4. Repeat this across the rug end, then trim the fringe to 2cm (¾in).

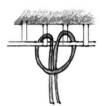

MINIATURE CHINESE RUG 2

This rug was also a small section adapted from a much larger carpet from the nineteenth century. The butterflies are again a symbol for conjugal harmony, and the flowers, which I think are a variation of the peony, stand for wealth and honour.

Working and making up the design

Follow the instructions for the rug above, but thread the needle with six strands of Anchor 887 for the fringe knots.

Materials
22-count canvas 23 x 15cm (9 x 6in)
Threads as listed

Thread required

	Anchor Stranded Cotton	Amount
	127	752.7cm (296⁶⁄₁₀in)
	123	633.0cm (249²⁄₁₀in)
	122	94.6cm (37²⁄₁₀in)
	121	39.8cm (15⁷⁄₁₀in)
	386	3458.7cm (1361⁷⁄₁₀in)

Design size	14.8 x 10.2cm (5⁹⁄₁₀ x 4in)
Stitch count	128 x 88
Number of strands	3

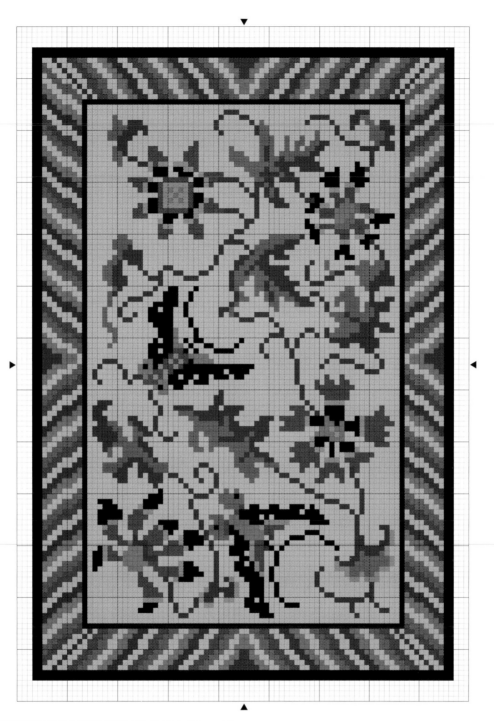

Thread required

	Anchor Stranded Cotton	Amount
■	403	712.5cm (280½in)
	887	2152.6cm (847½in)
■	879	542.8cm (213⁷⁄₁₀in)
	877	423.9cm (166⁵⁄₈in)
	843	72cm (253³⁄₁₀in)
	316	253.3cm (99⁷⁄₈in)
	326	372.6cm (146⁷⁄₁₀in)

Design size	9.7 x 14cm (3⁹⁄₁₀ x 5½in)
Stitch count	84 x 122
Number of strands	3

Chinese Painting

Over thousands of years Chinese artists have developed a particular style of painting. Sometimes they reproduce an accurate representation of the subject but often they aim to give a suggestion of the character with just a few brush strokes. The effect is achieved through a very disciplined, formal training, although it looks easy to the untrained eye.

Silk was used as a painting surface hundreds of years before paper, and bamboo and wood were also used. Xuan (rice) paper is the most commonly used type of paper, because this has a glue on the surface which makes it less absorbent and more suitable for inkwork. Brushes were made of hair, pointed and fastened into bamboo holders, and inks, which are an important material in Chinese painting, were a mixture of soot and glue. Ink was – and still is – made into solid sticks, which are freshly ground when needed. Before the eighteenth century, when commercial colours became available, painters used pigment from vegetable and mineral sources.

After the tenth century, many artists became interested in painting landscapes, so they mainly used ink washes on silk to make delicate paintings, and then made the outlines bolder. The Scenic Folding Fan (see page 84) is in this style.

Painters followed design formats such as scrolls, fan shapes and albums. I have shown some of these with the made-up articles in this book and fan formats, both round (screen) and folding, are included in the section on fans (see page 81). Album paintings are like divided pictures with either two or three parts of the painting separated by a frame or unpainted paper or silk. Scrolls could be hanging or vertical, similar to the bell-pulls on pages 28 and 93, or horizontal. Horizontal scrolls were also called hand scrolls because they were meant to be held in the hand and unrolled as they were read. They were not painted to be seen as a whole, but now many are displayed as such, so that the entire painting can be appreciated without damaging or wearing out the scroll. Thankfully, some rolled-up scrolls were wrapped in cloth and stored in sandalwood boxes, and larger scrolls were stored in tall ceramic jars with lids, so they have survived both the climate and insect damage. The astrological wall-hanging on page 18 is similar to these.

Three Pincushions Inspired by Paintings

I took three flower paintings in very different styles and adapted them for stitching. As I worked them they were just the right size to make pincushions, but would also make cushion centres if they were stitched on fabric with a smaller thread count.

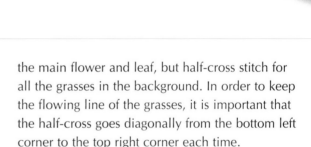

LOTUS PINCUSHION (1)

This beautiful design, stitched in subtle colours, would make an attractive small picture. I have chosen to work on a fine ecru fabric, using both full and half-cross stitch, in order to keep the delicacy. The design was closely based on a painting by Yun Shou P'ing who lived in the late seventeenth century and was regarded by many as the greatest Chinese painter of his time.

Working the design

Overcast the edges to prevent fraying, then work the design in the centre of the Aida using two strands over every thread. Use full cross stitch for the main flower and leaf, but half-cross stitch for all the grasses in the background. In order to keep the flowing line of the grasses, it is important that the half-cross goes diagonally from the bottom left corner to the top right corner each time.

Making up the design

Press well on the wrong side using a damp cloth. With right sides together, tack and stitch the backing to the embroidery leaving 5cm (2in) opening for turning through. Trim the excess seam fabric, clip the corners, then turn the right way. Stuff. I always use a polyester stuffing and lightly scent it with aromatic oils. Close the opening using slip stitch, then stitch the cord to the seam around the outside, allowing a loop at the bottom left-hand corner. Attach the tassel to the loop.

Materials

22-count ecru Aida 18cm (7in) square
Backing fabric 17cm (6½in) square
Cream cord 60cm (23½in)
Stuffing (either polyester or sawdust)
Tassel
Threads as listed

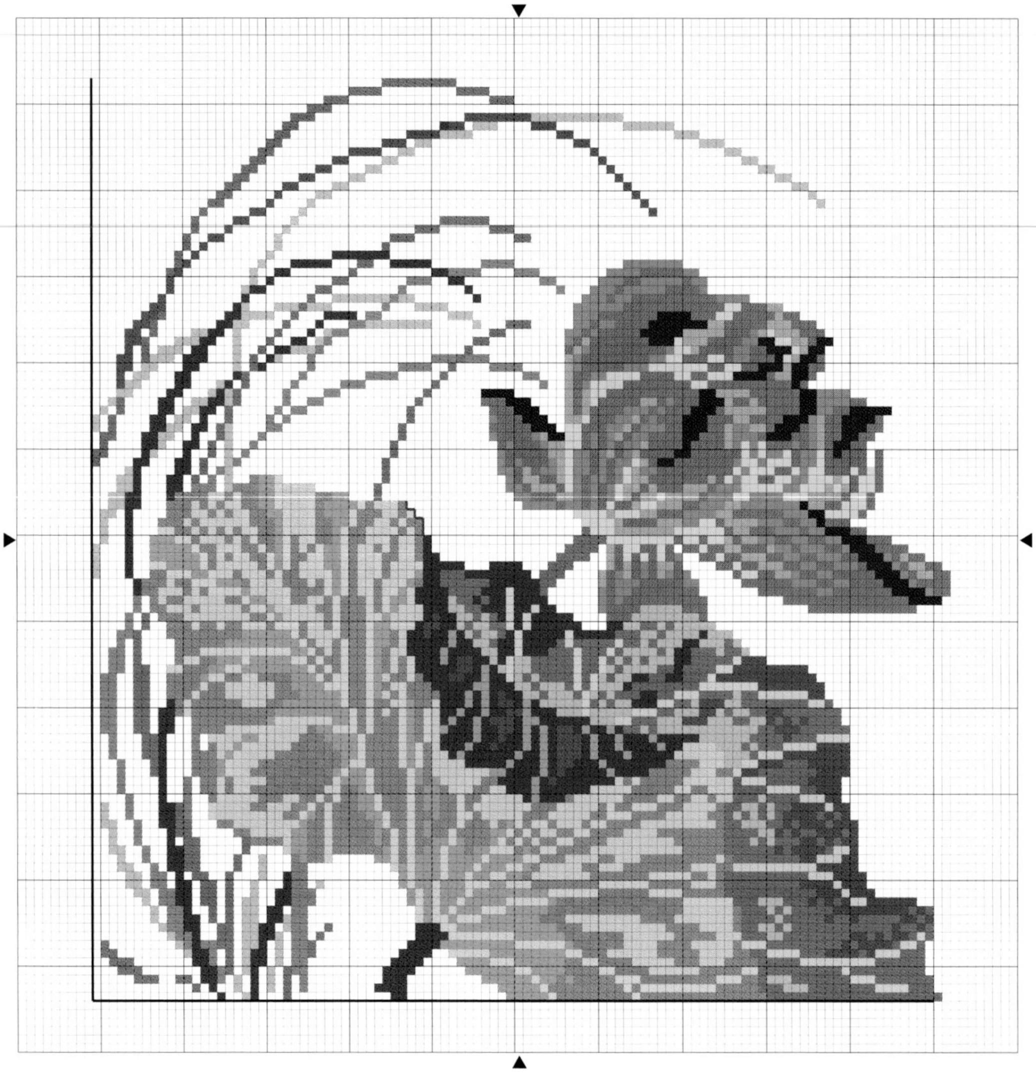

Design size	12 x 12.4cm (4 7/10 x 4 9/10in)
Stitch count	103 x 107
Number of strands	2

Thread required

	Anchor Stranded Cotton	Amount		Anchor Stranded Cotton	Amount
	390	169.1cm (66 6/10in)		843/853**	130.8cm (51 ½in)
	843	54.5cm (21 ½in)		854/843**	21.8cm (8 6/10in)
	843/845**	213cm (83 9/10in)		38	183cm (72in)
	845	22.7cm (8 9/10in)		36	50.7cm (20in)
	846	165.9cm (65 3/10in)		43/38**	43.3cm (17 1/10in)
	842/843**	120.2cm (47 3/10in)		36/275**	48.9cm (19 3/10in)
	854	237.2cm (93 4/10in)		36/38**	82.2cm (32 4/10in)
	845/846**	66.6cm (26 2/10in)		403* (1 Strand)	16cm (6 3/10in)
	842	6.8cm (2 7/10in)		846*	0.5cm (2/10in)
	852	147cm (57 9/10in)			

*Back stitch **Use 1 strand of each

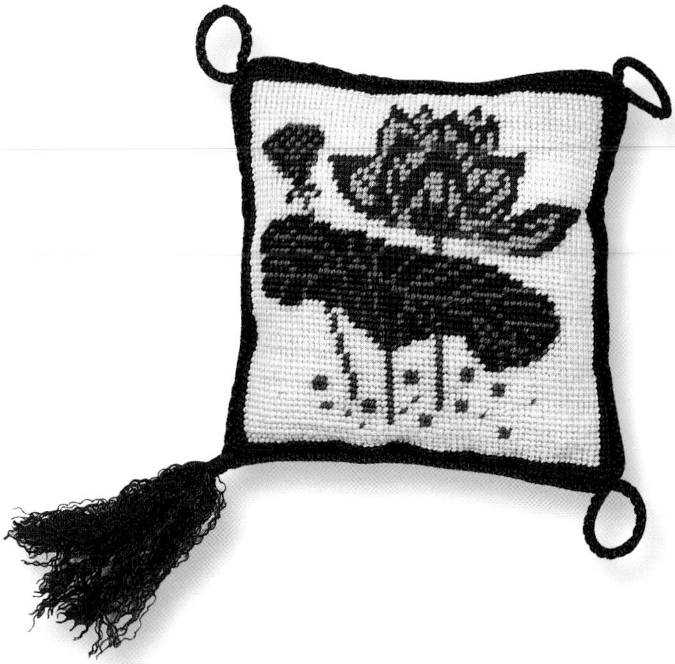

Lotus Pincushion (2)

This lotus design, from the late nineteenth century, is entirely different from the previous one and was originally used as a trademark created in watercolour and woodblock printing. The design lends itself to being stitched using wools and canvas.

Materials

14-count canvas 16cm (6¼in) square (preferably white, because of the cream background)

Backing fabric 16cm (6¼in) square

Deep red cord 80cm (31½in)

Polyester filling

Working the design

Stitch the design in the centre of the canvas using one strand wool and tent stitch.

Making up the design

Stretch the stitching back into shape, if necessary. Follow the instructions for Lotus Pincushion (1) on page 51, making sure you start stitching the cord from the bottom left-hand corner, leaving 8cm (3¼in) to be made into the tassel, and leaving loops at each corner. Bind the two ends of the cord together tightly, then unravel the single threads of the cord to form the tassel. Trim neatly.

Thread required

Anchor Tapestry Wool	Amount
9076	364cm (143 3/10in)
9080	1597.5cm (629in)
9174	105.6cm (41 6/10in)
8394	270.9cm (106 6/10in)
8400	409.8cm (161 3/10in)
8398	113.9cm (44 8/10in)
9204	91.7cm (36 1/10in)
8002	3097.9cm (1219 6/10in)

Design size	12 x 12cm (4 7/10 x 4 7/10in)
Stitch count	66 x 66
Number of strands	1 x Wool

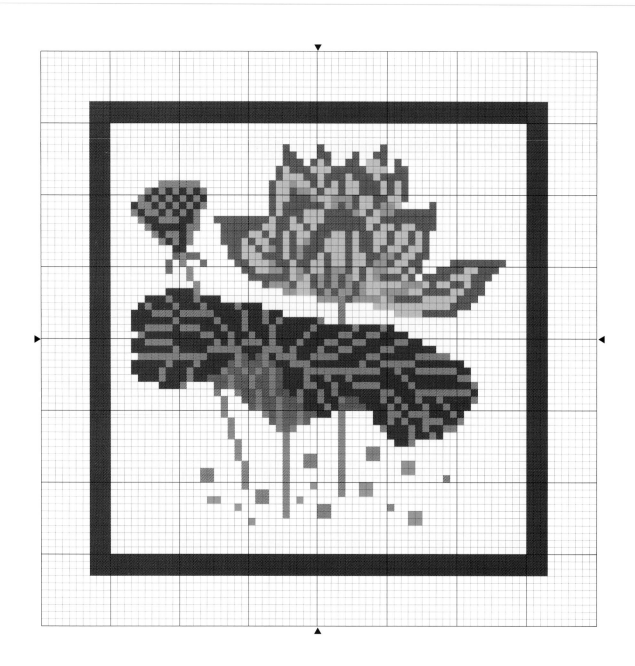

STYLIZED WATER LILY PINCUSHION

This design on this pincushion was inspired by an eighteenth-century painting. The black Jobelan and the cream beads give a sense of drama to the finished pincushion. I used black Jobelan for the backing as well as the front.

Working the design

Stitch the design in the centre of the Jobelan, using two strands over two threads, then add the beads.

Making up the design

Press well on the wrong side, using a damp cloth. Place right sides together and join the front and back, leaving a 5cm (2in) opening in the middle of one of the sides to allow for turning through. Turn to the right side, then, on the edges that are joined (i.e. not the opening) work a line of plain stitching 2cm (¾in) from the

side, to form a flanged edge. Stuff the centre with the polyester filling, then keeping the stuffing in the centre, join up the plain stitching and slip-stitch the opening closed. Fasten your choice of beads onto the corner using some black stranded cotton.

Materials

Black Jobelan 21.6cm (8½in) 2 x squares

25 Mill Hill beads 03021

Selection of beads for the corner (optional)

Polyester filling

Design size	12.9 x 12.2cm (5¹⁄₁₀ x 4⁸⁄₁₀in)
Stitch count	72 x 67
Number of strands	2

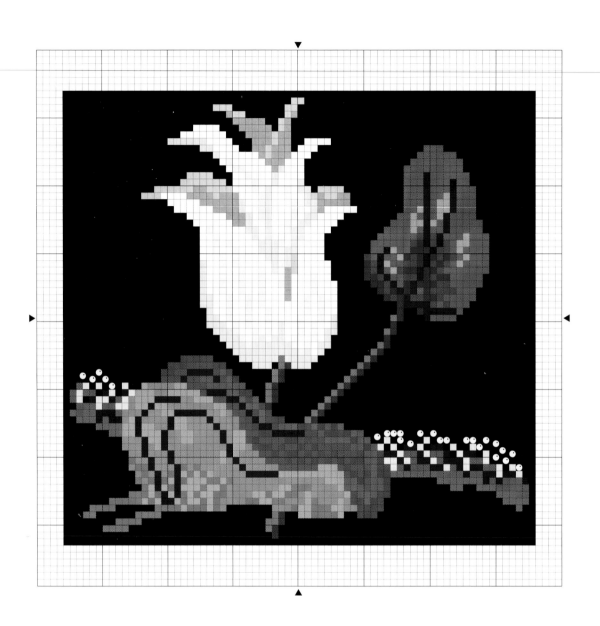

Thread required

	Anchor Stranded Cotton	Amount		Anchor Stranded Cotton	Amount
	Black Jobelan			241	86.1cm (33⅞in)
	298	35.2cm (13⅞in)		887/241**	65.8cm (25⅞in)
	298/White**	23.6cm (9⅜in)		245	30.1cm (11⅞in)
	1	163.9cm (64½in)		241/243**	49.5cm (19½in)
	926	40.7cm (16in)		243	133.4cm (52½in)
	246	72.7cm (28⅝in)		245/246**	35.7cm (14in)
	244	58.3cm (23in)		374	17.6cm (6⅞in)
	386 Perle Cotton	76.4cm (30⅛in)		Mill Hill 03021*	25

*Beads   **Use 1 strand of each

Dragons

Dragons are plentiful throughout Chinese mythology and are depicted in all art forms. Unlike the European dragons, they are usually fairly kind, good-natured creatures who rule over rain and thunder and look after the people, but they do have occasional fits of temper and cause violent storms and floods. Chinese dragons breathe clouds, not fire, and are thought to be a combination of a camel, demon, stag, cow, snake, carp, eagle and tiger. Every area of water is supposed to be guarded by a dragon, who lives in an underwater crystal palace with priceless treasures and eats opals and pearls. For this reason they are often portrayed as holding, playing with, or chasing a flaming pearl.

Dragons were representative of the Emperor and were depicted on his clothes, throne, furnishings and in every area of his palace. After 1783 only Imperial dragons were allowed to have five claws and anyone other than the emperor or the first prince had to have dragons with only four claws. When China became a republic in 1912, this decree ceased, and now five-clawed dragons can be used anywhere.

Tea-tray Set

The designs for these dragons originated during the Qing dynasty (1644–1912). The tray design was from some embroidery on an actor's costume depicting a door-god's armour. The teapot stand and tea-cosy developed from a design on an embroidered chair cover from the same dynasty. The dragon on these doesn't look quite as lively as the tray dragon, but it is shown holding the flaming pearl, whereas the tray dragon is chasing it among the clouds. The use of metallic thread adds a glint to the designs and they make a distinctive set, guaranteed to be a talking point among your friends.

DRAGON TRAY

Working the design

Overcast the edges to prevent fraying, then work the design in the centre of the fabric.

Making up

Press on the wrong side, using a damp cloth, then iron the Vilene onto the back of the work. Use the larger oval mount as a template and place your design in the centre; cut out the oval shape allowing 1cm (½in) extra all the way round. Fasten the design to the edges of the back of the smaller mount, then make up as per the instructions supplied with the tray.

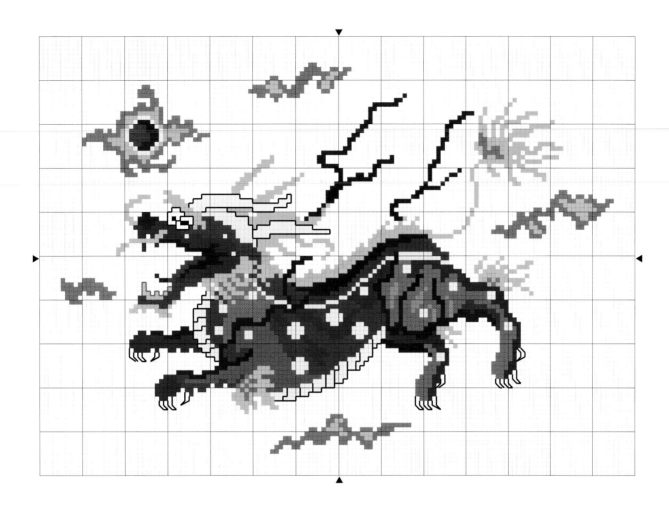

Design size	23.6 x 16.3cm (9³⁄₁₀ x 6⁴⁄₁₀in)
Stitch count	130 x 89
Number of strands	2

Materials

28-count Jobelan 35.5 x 28cm (14 x 11in) N.B. As this is worked over 2 threads, 14-count could be used instead.)

Iron-on Vilene 28 x 21cm (11 x 8¼in)

Tray: I used Framecraft tray MTRAY. This comes as shown, complete with mountboards and adhesive felt base. You will have to adjust the instructions if you are using a different tray (see 'Adapting Designs', page 4).

Threads as listed

Thread required

	Anchor Stranded Cotton	Amount
	403	1.4cm (½in)
	386	160.2cm (63¹⁄₁₀in)
	939	201cm (79¹⁄₁₀in)
	120	94.9cm (37⁴⁄₁₀in)
	46	74.6cm (29⁴⁄₁₀in)
	46/1014**	231.5cm (91²⁄₁₀in)
	214	12.5cm (4⁹⁄₁₀in)
	214/216**	146.8cm (57⁸⁄₁₀in)
	216/217**	74.1cm (29²⁄₁₀in)
	217	157.9cm (62²⁄₁₀in)
	218/217**	193.1cm (76in)
	Lamé 303†	253.8cm (99⁹⁄₁₀in)
	213	13cm (5¹⁄₁₀in)
	213/386**	44.5cm (17½in)
	403*	39.3cm (15½in)
	216* (on mouth)	2.1cm (⁸⁄₁₀in)

*Back stitch   **Use 1 strand of each   †Use 4 strands

Teapot Stand

Working the design

Overcast the edges to prevent fraying, then work the design in the centre of the fabric with two strands over every thread.

Making up

When the design is complete, press well on the wrong side of the stitching using a damp cloth. Iron on the Vilene, then follow the instructions for making up supplied with the teapot stand.

Thread required

	Anchor Stranded Cotton	Amount
	403	2.4cm (9/10in)
	386	69.3cm (27 3/10in)
	939	29.7cm (11 7/10in)
	120	59cm (23 2/10in)
	46	65.5cm (25 8/10in)
	46/1014**	39.6cm (15 6/10in)
	214	50.5cm (19 9/10in)
	215	14.7cm (5 8/10in)
	216/217**	58.7cm (23 1/10in)
	217	32.4cm (12 8/10in)
	218/217**	129.7cm (51in)
	Lamé 303†	100.3cm (39½in)
	213	21.8cm (8 6/10in)
	213/386**	43.3cm (17 1/10in)
	216	60.7cm (23 9/10in)
	403*	24cm (9 4/10in)
	216* (on mouth)	4.5cm (1 8/10in)

*Back stitch **Use 1 strand of each †Use 4 strands

Materials

19-count Easistitch 19cm (7½in) square

Iron-on Vilene 18cm (7in) square

Teapot stand: I used teapot stand WTS from Framecraft. You may have to adjust the measurements for a different stand

Threads as listed

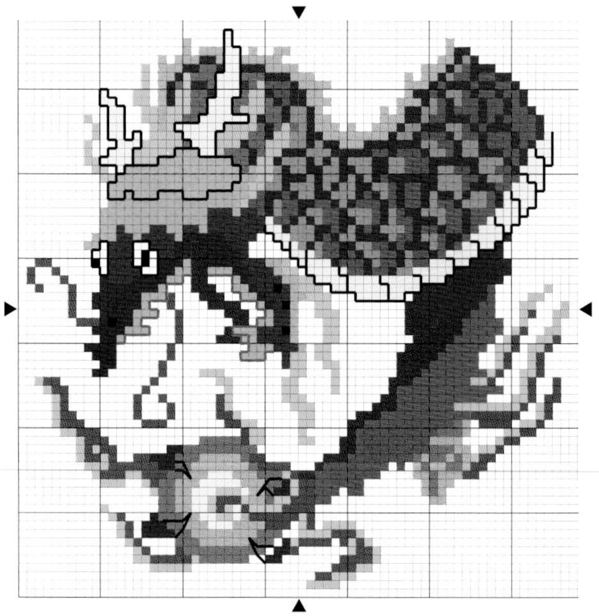

Design size	9 x 9cm (3.5 x 3.5in)
Stitch count	66 x 66
Number of strands	2

TEA-COSY

Working the design

Overcast the edges to prevent fraying, then work the design in the centre of the fabric using two strands over two threads.

Design size	12 x 12cm (4⅞₀ x 4⅞₀in)
Stitch count	66 x 66
Number of strands	2

Materials

White 28-count Jobelan 23cm (9in)

Green fabric for tea cosy: two pieces 41 x 34cm (16¼ x 13½in)

Iron-on Vilene 15cm (6in) circle

Heavy cotton for lining: two pieces 40.5 x 28cm (16 x 11in)

Medium-weight wadding: two pieces 38 x 26cm (15 x 10¼in)

Cord 58cm (23in) and tassels

Thread required

	Anchor Stranded Cotton	Amount
	403	3.2cm (1⅜₀in)
	386	94cm (37in)
	939	40.3cm (15⅞₀in)
	120	80.1cm (31½in)
	46	88.9cm (35in)
	46/1014**	53.7cm (21⅛₀in)
	214	68.5cm (27in)
	215	19.9cm (7⅞₀in)
	216/217**	79.6cm (31⅜₀in)
	217	44cm (17⅜₀in)
	218/217**	176cm (69⅜₀in)
	Lamé 303†	136.1cm (53⅝₀in)
	213	29.6cm (11⅞₀in)
	213/386**	58.8cm (23⅜₀in)
	216	82.4cm (32½in)
	403*	32.5cm (12⅝₀in)
	216* (on mouth)	2.4cm (6in)

*Back stitch   **Use 1 strand of each   †Use 4 strands

Making up

Enlarge the template to 38 x 30cm (15 x 12in). Add 3cm (1¼in) at the straight edge, then use this template to cut two pieces of green fabric and two pieces of lining. Cut two pieces of wadding the size of the template (without the 3cm/1¼in).

Press the embroidery on the wrong side, using a damp cloth, then iron the circle of Vilene onto the back of the design. Cut this out carefully. Stitch the circle onto one of the green shapes, placing it in the centre of the length and 8cm (3¼in) down from the top.

Stitch the cord round the edge of the circle to hide the edge, then add the tassels.

Pin and machine the green back and front of the tea-cosy, right sides together. Machine the curved side, keeping 1cm (½in) in from the edge, and add a short loop of cord in the centre at the top. Trim the seam, then turn the right way out. Machine the lining pieces, right sides together, then fasten the wadding to the two wrong sides of the lining. Fit the wadding and lining inside the tea-cosy, wrong sides together, so that the right side of the lining forms the inside of the cosy. Turn the bottom of the green fabric to the inside, and hem it over the edges of the wadded lining. Catch in the top of the lining to prevent it moving.

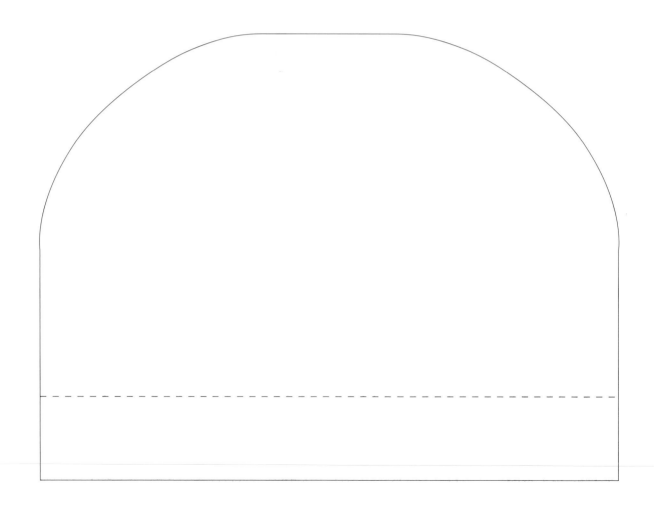

Ceramic Pot-lid

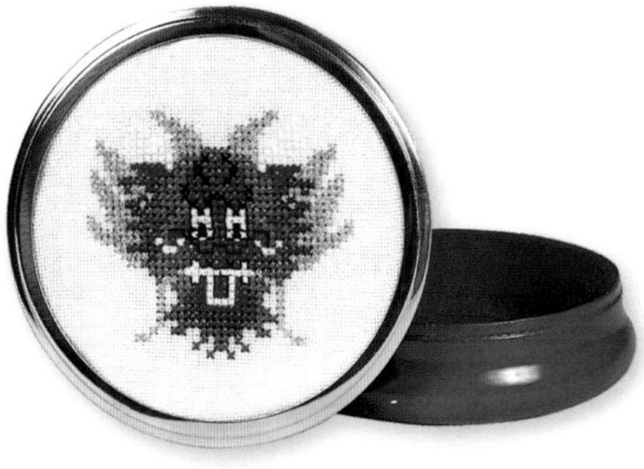

This bright green pot was perfect for the dragon head design that I found on an imperial dragon robe. The metallic gold threads match the gold embroidery on the robe.

Working the design

Overcast the edges to prevent fraying, then work the design in the centre using two strands and working over two threads.

Materials

32-count Jobelan 15cm (6in) square (as this is worked over two threads, 16-count could be substituted)

Iron-on Vilene 10cm (4in) circle

Lid with 10cm (4in) diameter

Threads as listed

Thread required

	Anchor Stranded Cotton	Amount
	403	10.5cm (4 1/10in)
	386 Perle	29.2m (11½in)
	245	60cm (23 6/10in)
	246	68.1cm (26 8/10in)
	Lamé 303†	65.6cm (25 8/10in)
	334	30.8cm (12 1/10in)
	1	6.9cm (2 7/10in)
	Lamé 300†	19.4cm (7 7/10in)
	403*	8.6cm (3 4/10in)
	1*	0.2cm (1/10in)

*Back stitch †Use 4 strands

Making up the design

Press the embroidery on the wrong side, using a damp cloth, then carefully iron the Vilene circle onto the back of the stitching, being sure to centre the design. Cut out the circle. Make up the lid as directed by the manufacturer.

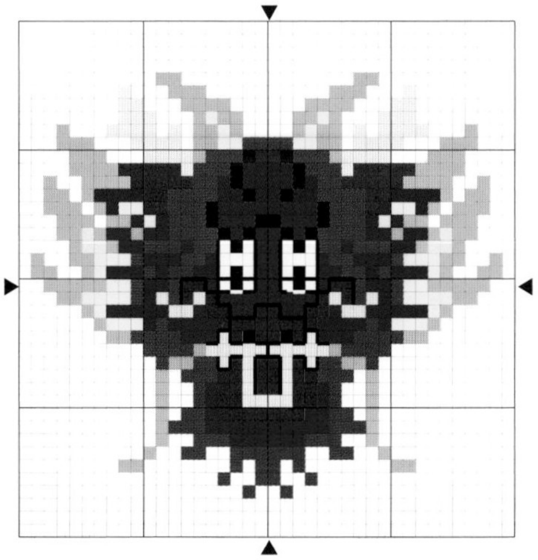

Design size	6.0 x 5.2cm (2 4/10 x 2 1/10in)
Stitch count	38 x 33
Number of strands	2

Phoenix

The phoenix is a mythical creature usually shown as a mixture of pheasant, peacock and stork. It is the queen of birds and represents the empress of China. The phoenix was thought to bring messages from the gods to the emperor in dreams while he slept. Phoenixes occur throughout Chinese art, often with tree peonies (Wu-t'ung) as these are depicted as their prime perching places. The seeds of the tree peony are edible and are eaten during the autumn Moon Festival in mooncakes, shaped in special moulds and decorated with auspicious characters.

Pair of Phoenix Pictures

I thought these would look well together, so have made one landscape and one portrait style; they need to be arranged so that the birds are looking at each other. The terracotta colours show up well on the black.

Working each design

Remember that Phoenix 1 is landscape and Phoenix 2 is portrait, so make sure that the fabric is the right way round for this. Overcast the edges to prevent fraying, then work the design in the centre of the fabric, using two strands over two threads.

Making up each design

Press on the wrong side using a damp cloth, then stretch and frame as you wish.

Materials

For each picture

28-count black Jobelan 35.5 x 25.5cm (14 x 10in). (The design is worked over two threads, so 14-count could be substituted)

Threads as listed

Thread required for pattern 1

Anchor Stranded Cotton	Amount
336	284.3cm (111$\frac{9}{10}$in)
338	192.2cm (75$\frac{7}{10}$in)
339	88cm (34$\frac{6}{10}$in)
1082	29.2cm (11$\frac{5}{10}$in)
400	126cm (49$\frac{6}{10}$in)
398	142.2cm (56in)
386	127.3cm (50$\frac{1}{10}$in)
341	2.2cm ($\frac{9}{10}$in)
341*	4.2cm (1$\frac{7}{10}$in)

*Back stitch

Design size	21 x 13.8cm (8$\frac{2}{10}$ x 5$\frac{4}{10}$in)
Stitch count	115 x 75
Number of strands	2

Thread required for pattern 2

Anchor Stranded Cotton	Amount
336	337.6cm (132$\frac{9}{10}$)
338	103.3cm (40$\frac{7}{10}$in)
339	182.4cm (71$\frac{8}{10}$in)
1082	43.1cm (17in)
400	233.8cm (92$\frac{1}{10}$in)
398	187.5cm (73$\frac{8}{10}$in)
386	184.3cm (72$\frac{6}{10}$in)
341	164.4cm (64$\frac{4}{10}$in)
341*	4.2cm (1$\frac{7}{10}$in)

*Back stitch

Design size	15 x 20.9cm (6 x 8$\frac{2}{10}$in)
Stitch count	84 x 115
Number of strands	2

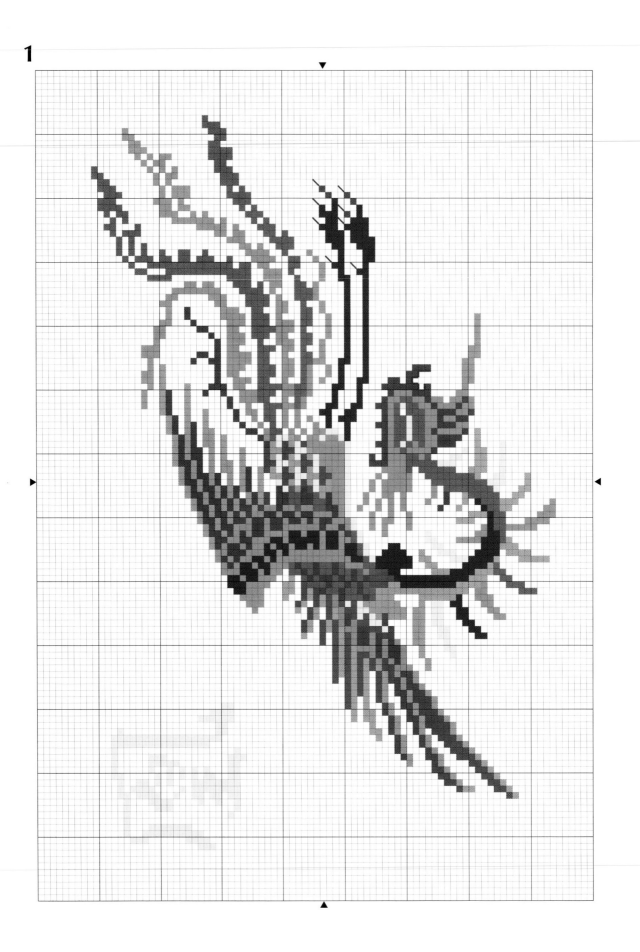

2

Gardens and Flowers

Chinese gardens also display the Chinese love of symbols. An ideal garden in China should have a hill or mountain, which may in fact only be a symbolic rock, water, either as a pond or running water, and a quiet area for meditating, which may be a pagoda or gazebo. Large gardens may have several of each of these. There are flowers in abundance throughout Chinese art, and their addition often gives symbolic meaning to the piece of work. I have given more details of these in appropriate places throughout the book.

Many flowers are linked to the seasons and months. By tradition there is a flower for each of the twelve lunar months. These are plum or prunus, magnolia, peach, rose, crab apple, tree peony, lotus, pomegranate, mallow, chrysanthemum, orchid and narcissus. In addition to their role here, the peony (spring), lotus (summer) chrysanthemum (autumn) and prunus (winter) are symbols of the four seasons, although occasionally bamboo is used for winter.

Peonies are known as the 'Flowers of Plenty' and are called 'hua wang' which means the King of Flowers. They are planted in gardens and in stone-edged flower beds as a summer attraction, but when the flowers die they are not cut down. Visitors to public gardens pay homage to these plants that grow, flower, fade and die in the same place.

It was considered important to have a lotus growing in gardens. Smaller gardens or houses with only a courtyard would have the plants growing in large bowls. In large lakes, paths were cut through the plants to allow small boats to pass through. The lotus was looked on as the symbol of Buddha and stands for purity. It grows from the muddy bottoms of lakes, but the flowers emerge unblemished and pure white. Buddha is thought to have survived this corrupt world to emerge pure and holy.

Chrysanthemums were originally grown for medicinal purposes, but they became known as an elixir for long life. There is a well-known story that the people of Nanyang in Central China drank all their water from a stream where hundreds of chrysanthemums grew. The people all lived to be over 100 years, and this longevity was thought to be because the chrysanthemum juices had filtered into the water.

The plum (prunus) represents winter, because in China it is the first flower to appear and heralds the arrival of spring. Plum blossom is often used to decorate blue and white porcelain jars which were given as presents in the New Year. The trees were grown for the blossom, rather than the fruit.

Some plants are grouped together and shown in the same design. 'The Four Lords' are prunus, orchid, bamboo and chrysanthemum. 'Friends of Winter' are pine, bamboo and prunus. The 'Three Plenties' or 'Three Abundances' are a peach, pomegranate and a strange citrus fruit called the 'Buddha's Hand Citron'. They are collectively called the 'Three Plenties' because the combination of peaches for longevity, pomegranates for plenty of sons, and the citrus fruit for abundant happiness would give a full and happy life.

Even in the cemeteries the planting is ordered. Pines stand for the ruler, thuja for princes, poplars for commoners and there are different trees for scholars and governors.

Several more plants are dealt with in the text accompanying the designs and in the section on Auspicious Characters (see page 10).

Three Friends
Pot-pourri Cushion

Prunus, pine and bamboo are found together throughout all areas of Chinese design, and are known as the 'Three Friends of Winter' or the 'Friends of the Cold Season' because they are plants of the winter. Pines and bamboo are evergreen and the prunus flowers very early in the spring in China, flowering even if there is a metre or so of snow on the ground.

I have used some designs from porcelain dishes and bowls from the fifteenth and sixteenth century to make the pattern for this pot-pourri cushion.

Working the design

Overcast the edges to prevent fraying, then work the design in the centre of the fabric using two strands of cotton (three for the back stitch) over every thread.

Making up the design

Press well on the wrong side using a damp cloth. Iron the circle of Vilene centrally on the back of the stitching, then carefully cut it out. Tack, then fasten, using a zigzag stitch in the centre of one of the backing pieces. Carefully stitch the lace around the Aida to cover the edge then, with right sides facing, stitch the two backing pieces together to form a 14cm (5½in) square. Leave an opening of 5cm (2in) to allow it to be turned through. Turn it the right way, stuff, and slip stitch the opening to close it. Fasten the loop of ribbon at the top, then decorate as you wish – I hung a bead from the bottom on a short length of ribbon.

Materials

22-count Aida 18cm (7in) square

Backing, 2 x 15cm (6in) squares (I used dark blue to match the threads)

Lace, 45cm (18in), that will stretch round a circle (the one I have used here is called 'Church Windows' for obvious reasons, and is one that I use a lot)

Bows and beads, or a tassel to decorate, and a small piece of ribbon for a hanging loop

Iron-on Vilene: 10cm (4in) circle

Polyester filling and perfume oil

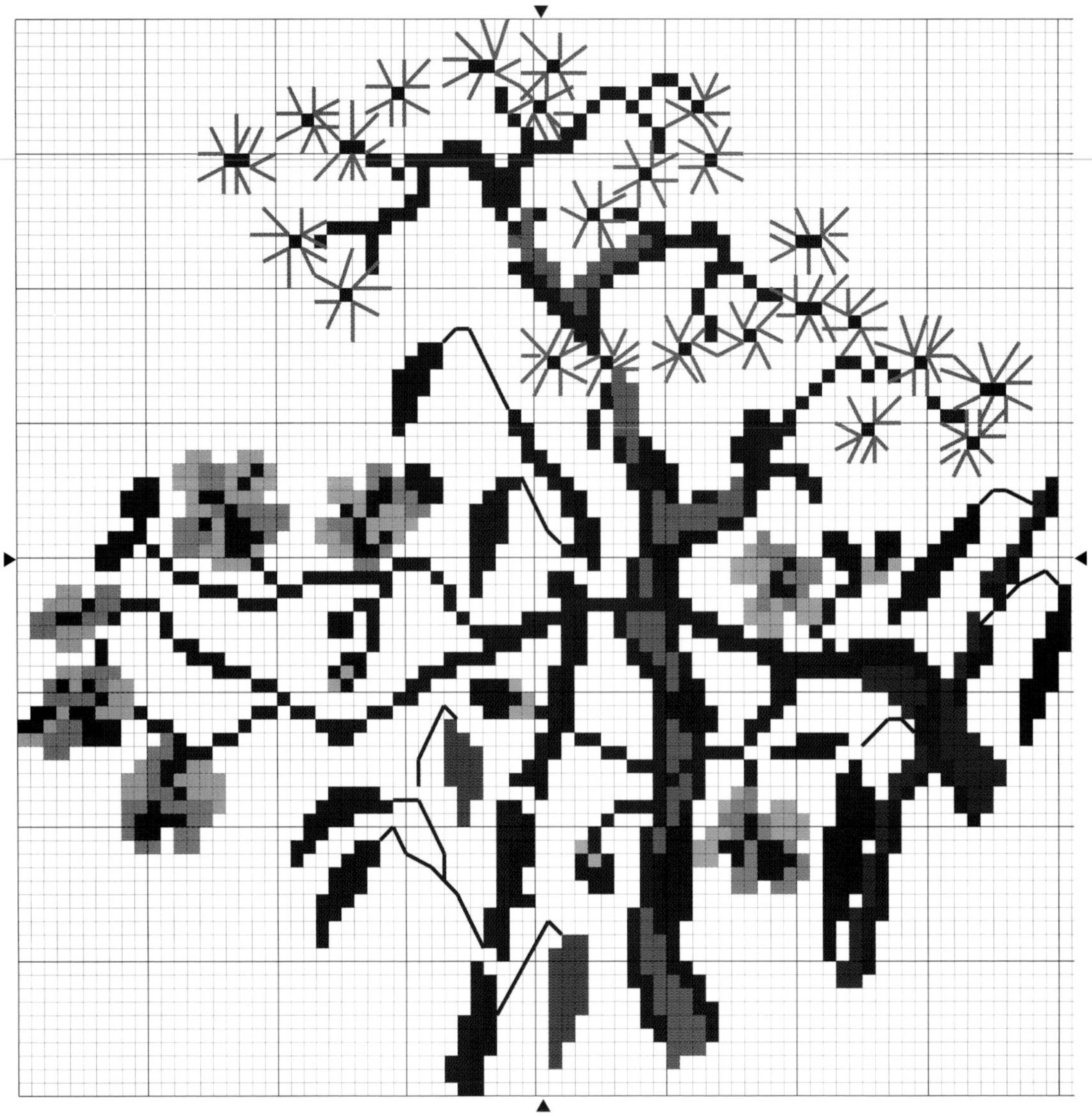

Design size	9.4 x 9.2cm (3 7/10 x 3 6/10in)
Stitch count	81 x 80
Number of strands	2

Thread required

	Anchor Stranded Cotton	Amount
	150	113.7cm (44 8/10in)
	150/139**	163.5cm (64 4/10in)
	139	21.2cm (8 4/10in)
	139/137**	11.5cm (4 5/10in)
	137	30.6cm (12 1/10in)
	137/136**	34.5cm (13 6/10in)
	136	38.9cm (15 3/10in)
	150*	4.8cm (1 9/10in)
	137*†	34.3cm (13 5/10in)

*Back stitch †Use 3 strands **Use 1 strand of each

Chinese Buildings

While I was researching this book I realized that I couldn't ignore the buildings, especially the magnificent and decorative temples, palaces and pagodas which for many people symbolize Chinese architecture. I took a number of different buildings, then used actual details from them to design a pagoda picture.

Many of the temples and palaces were built in this tiered style, with wonderfully decorated woodwork, clay-tiled roofs and marble balustrades. Most of them are painted gold or orange, as gold and orange mean joy. Enclosed walled courtyards were a feature of the houses of the important families, and either within these, or in the gardens, building a pagoda was thought to bring good luck to the place. Mythical creatures were commonly placed on the eaves of buildings, to frighten away harmful spirits that might wish to enter, and tiles of the directional gods were placed on the roofs with their corresponding images: East was a green dragon, South a scarlet bird, West a white tiger, North a dark warrior and the centre was a yellow dragon. The dark warrior is often shown by a tortoise, sometimes with a snake wrapped round it.

Houses must be aligned correctly, as must their contents, to ensure harmony. The art of learning to live in harmony with our surroundings, whether at home, in the garden, in the office, or in public places is called feng shui. According to its principles, each of the twelve Chinese astrological animals is attributed with a particular element, so that water (North) is pig, rat and ox; metal (West) is dog, cockerel and monkey; fire (South) is goat, horse and snake; and wood (East) is tiger, dragon and rabbit.

To align a house, or indeed any building, a specialist geomancer is called in who uses a geomantic compass, called a luo pan, to position the building in relation to Heaven, Earth and Man and make it harmonious. This also involves trigrams which again relate to yin and yang. The yin–yang symbols are frequently surrounded by the Eight Trigrams. These are arrangements of three lines broken up in various different ways to symbolize heaven, wind, water, mountains, earth, thunder, fire and clouds.

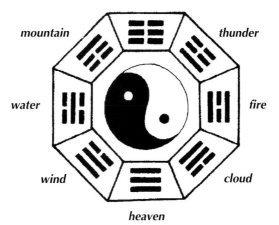

earth

mountain

thunder

water

fire

wind

cloud

heaven

Pagoda Picture

Working the design

Overcast the edges to prevent fraying, then work the design in the centre of the fabric using two strands of cotton over two threads. Add the back stitch when the cross stitch is complete.

Making up the design

Press well on the wrong side using a damp cloth. Stretch on hardboard and frame as you wish.

Materials

28-count Jobelan 51 x 43.5cm (20 x 17in)

Threads as listed

Design size	42.1 x 28.8cm (16 6/10 x 11 4/10in)
Stitch count	232 x 159
Number of strands	2

Thread required

Anchor Stranded Cotton	Amount
376/378**	514.9cm (202 7/10in)
378/379**	671.4cm (264 3/10in)
848	782.6cm (308 1/10in)
850	117.6cm (46 3/10in)
779	111.1cm (43 8/10in)
851	226.0cm (89in)
842	55.6cm (21 9/10in)
843	291.7cm (114 9/10in)
845	372.3cm (146 6/10in)
379	271.4cm (106 8/10in)
894	113.9cm (44 8/10in)
1027	1281.7cm (504 6/10in)
896/897**	126.9cm (50in)
897	851.6cm (335.3/10in)
Lamé 303†	120.4cm (47 4/10in)
896/897**	408.9cm (161in)
904	142.2cm (56in)
878	219.5cm (86 4/10in)
379*	52.6cm (20 7/10in)
851*	55.3cm (21 8/10in)
897*	7.9cm (3 1/10in)
845*	43.2cm (17in)
Lamé 303*†	12.8cm (5in)
878*	97.1cm (38 2/10in)
904*	53.7cm (21 1/10in)

*Back stitch †Use 4 strands **Use 1 strand of each

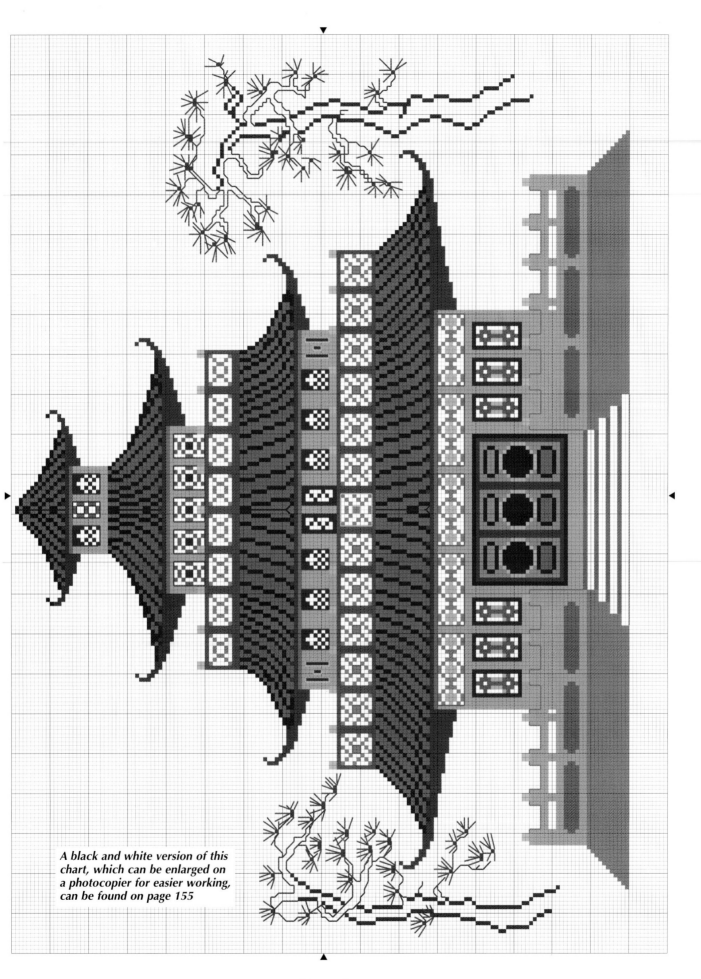

A black and white version of this chart, which can be enlarged on a photocopier for easier working, can be found on page 155

Chinese Games

I have chosen to use designs connected with just two games particular to China – chess and mah-jong. Chess is the most popular game in China and, in 1975, the Chinese government published and distributed nearly half a million copies of the rules to encourage people to play. The Chinese version of chess varies from the European game. It is played as a game involving armies with a fortress, mandarins and elephants, and a central river that elephants are not allowed to cross.

Mah-jong originated in Shanghai over a century ago, as a development from playing-cards. Originally designed for fortune-telling, the cards are now used for a game which is similar to rummy, and often the playing cards have been superseded by 144 domino-like tiles many of which have been beautifully carved from bone, ivory or even mother-of-pearl. Affordable sets now are more likely to be made of plastic. It follows traditional Chinese ideas with honour tiles of dragons and winds, especially the east wind, flowers and seasons. Mah-jong is sometimes known as the 'Game of Four Winds' or 'Matchay', which means 'sparrow', because of the clicking sound of the tiles as they are played.

Chess-board

This is both a decorative and practical piece to create, and although it involves quite a lot of stitching it splits up nicely into small areas, which can be completed fairly quickly.

I have used sixteen flower designs from old Chinese textiles to form the 'coloured' squares, and added a border from a ceramic bowl. Using 28-count Jobelan and working over two threads gives a suitable size for actually playing a game, but it could be stitched on a smaller count fabric and framed as a picture.

Working the design

Overcast the edges to prevent fraying, then stitch the design in the centre of the fabric using two strands and working over two threads.

Making up the design

Press the embroidery on the wrong side, using a damp cloth, then stretch it over a piece of hardboard 40.5cm (16in) square. Now frame it as a picture, using a wide picture-frame moulding but, for safety, use acrylic rather than glass. Stick a 42cm (16½in) square of felt on the back, to prevent it from scratching the table top. You can also fasten miniature wooden feet – such as those used for dolls' furniture – at each corner if you wish.

Thread required

	Anchor Stranded Cotton	Amount
	403	3691.5cm (1453 3/10in)
	306	211.2cm (83 1/10in)
	878	258.4cm (101 7/10in)
	876/878*	52.8cm (20 8/10in)
	876	161.1cm (63 4/10in)
	337	602.0cm (237in)
	5975	1392cm (548in)
	117	352.8cm (138 9/10in)
	122	802.9cm (316 1/10in)
	117/Cream*	183.4cm (72 2/10in)
	45	1185.4cm (466 7/10in)
	45/5975*	278.8cm (109 7/10in)
	386	201.9cm (79 5/10in)
	337/Cream*	237.1cm (93 3/10in)
	214	18.5cm (7 3/10in)

*Use 1 strand of each

A black and white version of this chart, which can be enlarged on a photocopier for easier working, can be found on page 156

Design size	38.8 x 38.8cm (15⁷⁄₁₀ x 15⁷⁄₁₀in)
Stitch count	214 x 214
Number of strands	2

Materials

28-count Jobelan 50cm x 50cm (19½in x 19½in)

Threads: Anchor Stranded Cotton

Five skeins of 403 (black), two each of 5975 and 45, and one each of 306, 876, 878, 337, 117, 122, 386 and 214

Mah-jong Games Cloth and Coasters

a

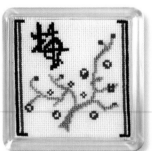

b

I used a selection of pieces from an actual game to design this matching games cloth and coasters which could, of course, be used for other things apart from playing mah-jong. As winds are such an important part of the mah-jong game, one of the coasters is a wind tile with the wind direction symbols [a]. The flowers, known as the Four Lords, are representative of the seasons: spring is a plum branch [b], summer is an orchid [c], autumn is a chrysanthemum [d] and winter is bamboo [e]. The sixth coaster is a character tile [f] showing the number six and the Chinese symbol for 'wan' which stands for 10,000, so this tile in the game would be worth 60,000. The circle tile on the cloth corner represents cash or coins.

c

d

e

f

GAMES CLOTH

Working and making up the design

Turn a 2cm (¾in) hem all the way round the edges. Measure 3.8cm (1½in) along the diagonal of the corner and mark with a pin. This is the square represented by the outline on the chart. Work the design using two strands over two threads, then press on the wrong side using a damp cloth.

<table>
<tr><td>Materials</td></tr>
</table>

Materials

28-count Jobelan 89cm (35in) square (I used NJ429.63)

Design size	13.4 x 13.4cm (5³/₁₀ x 5³/₁₀in)
Stitch count	74 x 74
Number of strands	2

Thread required

	Anchor Stranded Cotton	Amount
■	403	184.3cm (72⁵/₁₀in)
■	266	9.7cm (3⁸/₁₀in)
■	13	282.5cm (111²/₁₀in)
	1 (White)	151.9cm (59⁸/₁₀in)

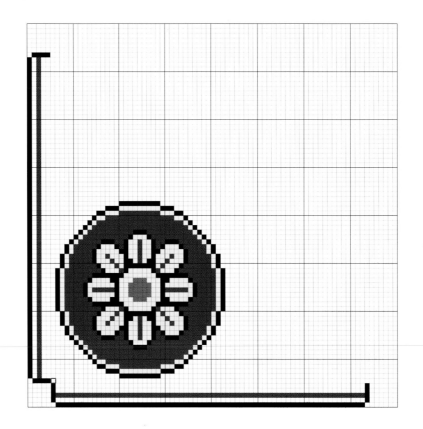

Coasters

Working the design

Overcast the edges to prevent fraying, then work the designs in the centre of each piece of fabric using two strands over two threads.

Making up the designs

Press on the wrong side using a damp cloth, then iron a square of Vilene on the back of each design. Now trim the stitching carefully, using sharp scissors, leaving one extra thread all the way round. The Vilene should keep the edges firm. Insert the stitching into the coaster following the manufacturer's instructions.

Materials

For each coaster: an 8cm (3⅛in) square coaster, 18-count Aida 10cm (4in) square, iron-on Vilene 8cm (3¼in) square.

Threads: Anchor Stranded Cotton

To stitch one corner of the cloth and six coasters you will need two skeins of 403 (black), and one skein each of 266, 13 and 1 (white)

Design size	7.5 x 7.5cm (3 x 3in)
Stitch count	54 x 54
Number of strands	2

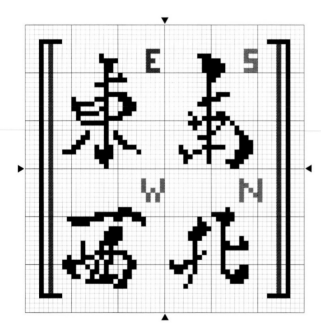

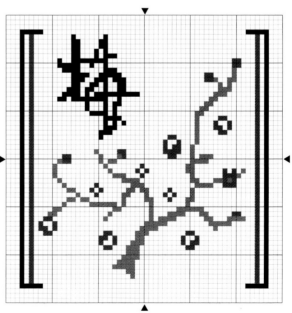

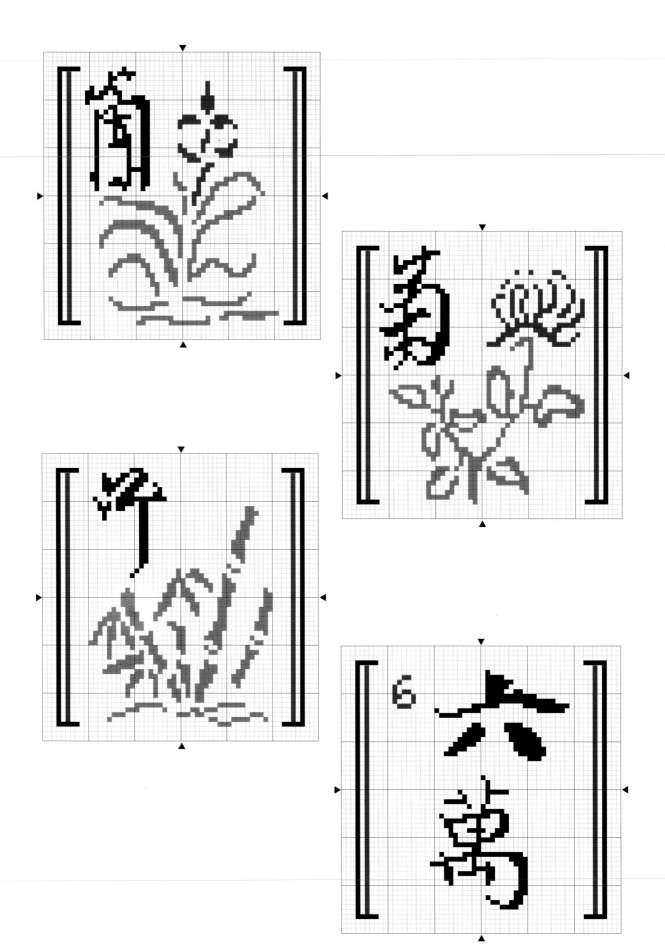

Fans

Fans are thought to have originated in Korea; they then went to Japan and came to China during the tenth century. They were made from paper, bamboo, silk or wood. Many of them were made from untreated sandalwood; as the scent of this wood becomes stronger with age, the fans helped to scent clothes in cupboards and drawers. Instead of being painted, these fans often have a design of punched holes.

Fans come in two main forms: folding fans and screen fans, which are also called palace fans. I have shown a screen fan being held in the picture of a Chinese lady. The oval shape would be painted flat then fastened to a vertical stick made of bamboo or ivory.

Folding fans are usually made with two almost semi-circular pieces of silk or paper pressed into folds. Thin bamboo staves fasten inside to give support to the fan. One of the two folding fans shown in the fan pictures is a wooden fan, shaped and decorated like a peacock. Peacocks represent beauty in China, and are supposed to show off when they see something or someone beautiful. Chinese craftsmen often create objects like fans, lanterns and kites in representational shapes of butterflies, tigers, birds, dragons and fish.

The other fan is a scenic fan which would be painted in Chinese fashion to represent the landscape. Many people took their favourite fans out of the supports and placed them in special albums to preserve them. Some Chinese artists design their work in a fan shape, even if the completed painting is not to be made into a fan at all. This is called fan painting.

Peacock Fan Picture

This is a precise piece with bright colours enhanced by the use of metallic thread and sequins. Coton à broder is used to give the duller look of the bamboo. I added a tassel made from left-over threads from this picture.

Working the design

Overcast the edges to prevent fraying, then stitch the design in the centre of the fabric using two strands and working over two threads with stranded cotton and one strand over two threads of coton à broder. Work the back stitch after the cross stitching is complete.

Making up the design

Press the embroidery on the wrong side using a damp cloth. Stitch on the sequins using a single strand of green. Thread the tassel through to the back and secure. Stretch the embroidery over a piece of board 40cm x 32cm (15.5in x 12.5in) and frame as required.

Materials

28-count Jobelan 45cm x 38cm (18in x 15in)
Eight green, 5mm sequins
Tassel – optional
Threads as listed

Design size	35.0 x 21.4cm (13⁸⁄₁₀ x 8⁴⁄₁₀in)
Stitch count	193 x 118
Number of strands	2

Thread required

Anchor Stranded Cotton	Amount
403	752cm (296¹⁄₁₀in)
150	113.4cm (44⁷⁄₁₀in)
386	1031.7cm (406²⁄₁₀in)
Coton à broder 887**	405.6cm (159⁷⁄₁₀in)
Coton à broder 386**	493.6cm (194³⁄₁₀in)
149	475.6cm (187²⁄₁₀in)
Lamé 322 (Metallic)†	14.8cm (5⁸⁄₁₀in)
Lamé 320 (Metallic)†	32.9cm (12⁹⁄₁₀in)
188/149**	289.4cm (113⁹⁄₁₀in)
1089	436.2cm (171⁷⁄₁₀in)
188	571.4cm (225in)
205	396cm (156²⁄₁₀in)
253	100cm (39⁴⁄₁₀in)
245	268.1cm (105⁶⁄₁₀in)
204	232.5cm (91⁵⁄₁₀in)
188*	3.5cm (1⁴⁄₁₀in)
1*	0.5cm (²⁄₁₀in)
403*	9.7cm (3⁸⁄₁₀in)
Green Sequin	

*Back stitch †Use 3 strands **Use 1 strand of each

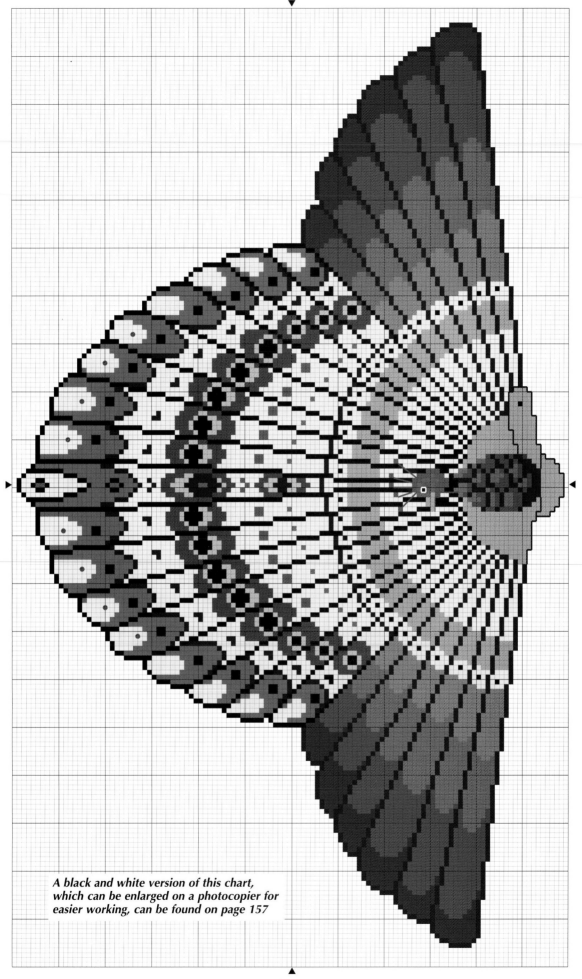

*A black and white version of this chart,
which can be enlarged on a photocopier for
easier working, can be found on page 157*

Scenic Folding Fan

This would probably be painted on paper or possibly on silk. It has subtle changes of colour that are achieved in the stitching by using mixed colours in the needle. This fan is painted in Chinese landscape form and you'll find more details of this in the section on Chinese Painting (see page 50). I have added a chunky tassel, which comes forward over the framing, so the picture cannot have glass in the front. If you want to have glass, use a smaller tassel like the one shown in the peacock fan.

Working the design

Overcast the edges to prevent fraying, then stitch the design in the centre of the fabric using two strands and working over two threads.

Making up the design

Press the embroidery on the wrong side, using a damp cloth. Fasten the tassel through from the front to the back and secure. Stretch the embroidery over a board 44 x 35.5cm (17.5 x 14in) and frame as you please.

Thread required

	Anchor Stranded Cotton	Amount
	372	568.6cm (223⅗in)
	360	179.7cm (70⅞in)
	386	464.9cm (183in)
	779/386**	91.2cm (35⅞in)
	850/386**	120.9cm (47⅗in)
	887	151.9cm (59⅘in)
	887/386**	46.3cm (18⅕in)
	889	212.5cm (83⅗in)
	340	17.6cm (6⅞in)
	904	387.1cm (152⅖in)
	887/852**	2106.4cm (829⅗in)
	842/852**	252.4cm (99⅖in)
	852	108.4cm (42⅗in)
	386/850**	441.8cm (173⅘in)
	877/215**	395.0cm (155⅗in)
	877/888**	225.5cm (88⅘in)
	843	113.0cm (44⅖in)
	843/842**	214.9cm (84⅗in)
	340/843**	170.9cm (67⅖in)
	779/843**	220.4cm (86⅘in)
	843/877**	209.8cm (82⅗in)
	403*	1.9cm (⅘in)
	360*	51.4cm (20⅕in)

*Back stitch   **Use 1 strand of each

Materials

28-count Jobelan 51cm x 43.5cm (20in x 17in)
Tassel of your choice
Threads as listed

Design size	38.3 x 23cm (15¹⁄₁₀ x 9in)
Stitch count	211 x 126
Number of strands	2

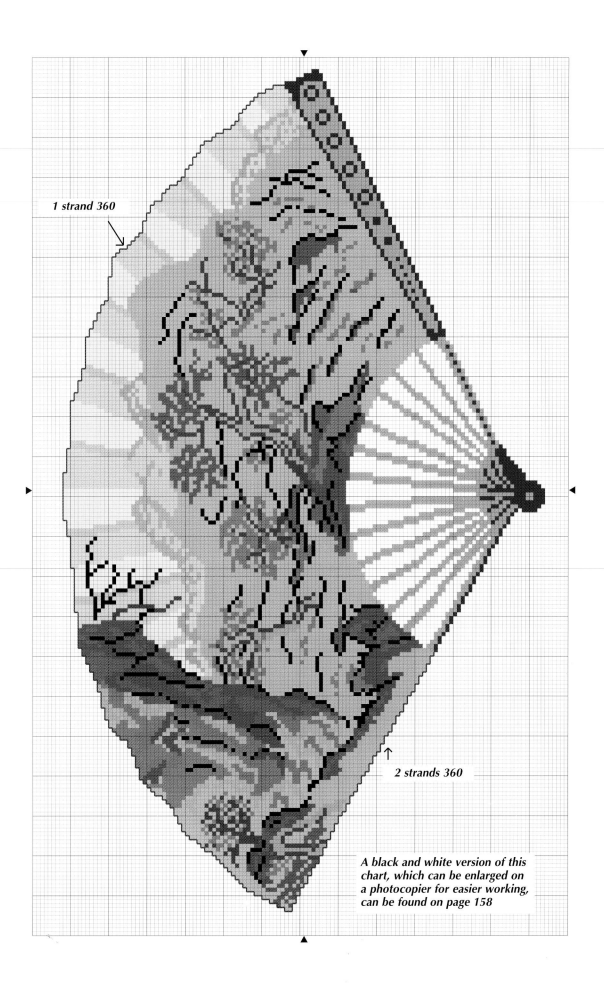

1 strand 360

↑
2 strands 360

A black and white version of this
chart, which can be enlarged on
a photocopier for easier working,
can be found on page 158

Lady Holding a Screen Fan

This involves a lot of work, but it is a beautiful picture when completed with beads, flowers and metallic thread. The large area of detailed stitching helps to create the flowing effect of the dress. Add the beads and flowers once all the stitching is complete.

Until the second half of the nineteenth century there were very rigid rules of dress code. In China certain colours and designs specified the importance of the wearer, and yellow was the imperial colour. Even the colour of a ribbon had to match the rank of the person wearing it. The empress had five strings of pearls, but nobody else was allowed to have more than two. Court ladies, too, had a very strict code of dress. They usually had their hair fastened with elaborate hairpins, many of which looked alive as the ladies moved their heads.

Working the design

Overcast the edges to prevent fraying, then work the design in the centre of the fabric. Note: the lady is worked in full cross stitch, but the picture on the fan is in half-cross stitch.

Work the cross stitch and half-cross stitch first, then the back stitch. Press on the wrong side using a damp cloth then add the beads. Use one strand cotton and a beading needle, and work a half-cross stitch through each bead.

Making up

Press lightly on the wrong side again, if necessary, then stitch the flowers in place, one in the hair and one at the base of the beaded cream band.

Stretch over a board and frame to your requirements. I left a wide margin and added a cream mount, because it shows off the stitching to great effect.

Materials

32-count fabric 38 x 56cm (15 x 22in)

(N.B. As the design is stitched over two threads, 16-count fabric will give the same result)

Two small ribbon flowers

161 x Mill Hill Glass Seed beads 02003

Threads as listed

Thread required

	Anchor Stranded Cotton	Amount
	403	319.3cm ($125\frac{7}{10}$in)
	228	162.9cm ($64\frac{1}{10}$in)
	242	160.4cm ($63\frac{2}{10}$in)
	6	924.2cm ($363\frac{9}{10}$in)
	8	235cm ($92\frac{5}{10}$in)
	9	186cm ($73\frac{2}{10}$in)
	10	1017.4cm ($400\frac{5}{10}$in)
	11	306.3cm ($120\frac{6}{10}$in)
	13/11†††	490.3cm (193in)
	13	169.4cm ($66\frac{7}{10}$in)
	8/9	131.3cm ($51\frac{7}{10}$in)
	403/372†††	16.2cm ($6\frac{4}{10}$in)
	Lamé 303†	24.7cm ($9\frac{7}{10}$in)
	390	186.4cm ($73\frac{4}{10}$in)
	390/372†††	51.9cm ($20\frac{4}{10}$in)
	386	530.4cm ($208\frac{8}{10}$in)
	235	370.3cm ($145\frac{8}{10}$in)
	848	440.4cm ($173\frac{4}{10}$in)
	369	153.2cm ($60\frac{3}{10}$in)
	343	77.4cm ($30\frac{1}{2}$in)
	1042	91.2cm ($35\frac{9}{10}$in)
	876	2.4cm (1in)
	10/11†††	31.6cm ($12\frac{4}{10}$in)
	379	36.9cm ($14\frac{5}{10}$in)
	403*††	26.1cm ($10\frac{3}{10}$in)
	11*	8.8cm ($3\frac{1}{2}$in)
	Mill Hill 02003**	

*Back stitch **Beads †Use 3 strands ††Use 1 strand

†††Use 1 strand of each

Design size	25 x 41.6cm ($9\frac{9}{10}$ x $16\frac{4}{10}$in)
Stitch count	159 x 262
Number of strands	2

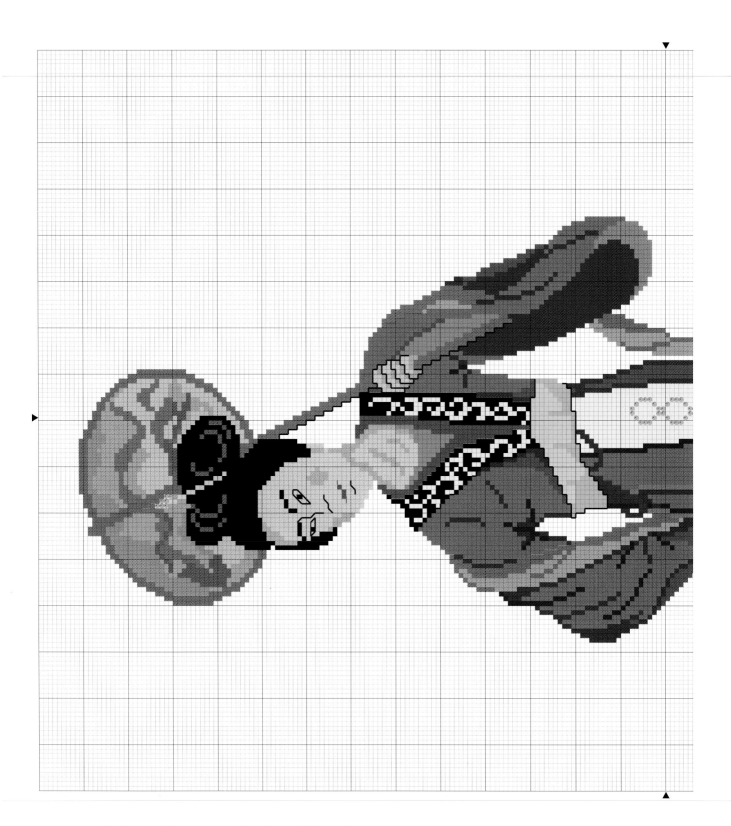

A black and white version of this chart, which can be enlarged on a photocopier for easier working, can be found on pages 159–60

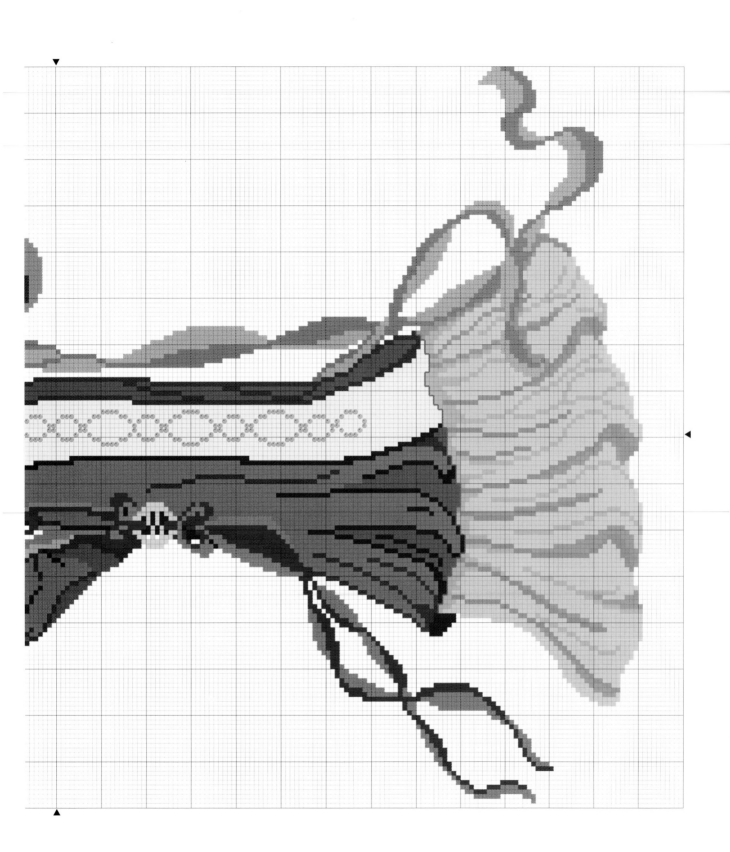

FURTHER DESIGNS

Further Designs

This section provides a collection of designs and ideas for you to interpret in your own way.

Brass Pot-lid

This design came from a painted china bottle and, worked on 28-count Jobelan over two threads, fits a 10cm (4in) lid. The gold lamé (worked with three threads) matches the gold edge of the lid on the pot. When complete, back the stitching with iron-on Vilene before fixing it into the lid.

Design size	6 x 6.5cm (2⁴⁄₁₀ x 2⁵⁄₁₀in)
Stitch count	33 x 36
Fabric count	14 holes per inch
Number of strands	2

Thread required

	Anchor Stranded Cotton	Amount
	843	23.2cm (9¹⁄₁₀in)
	89	101.4cm (39⁹⁄₁₀in)
	86	80.1cm (31½in)
	86/White†	74.1cm (29²⁄₁₀in)
	Gold Lamé 303††	28.2cm (11¹⁄₁₀in)
	123	13cm (5¹⁄₁₀in)
	Mill Hill 03059*	

*Beads   †Use 1 strand of each   ††Use 3 strands

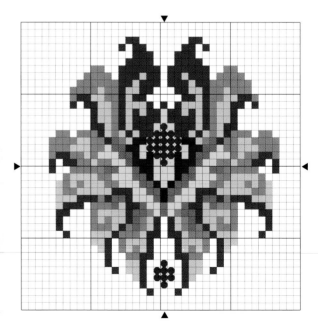

Bird and Flower Bell-pull

This is one of the larger designs, but it splits up into smaller sections which can be completed before moving on to the next area, so it is enjoyable to work. When completed, it makes a beautiful hanging – well worth the effort.

The parrot at the top was from an ink and watercolour design on a silk scroll from the Northern Song dynasty (960–1127), and the two lower birds were from palace fans from the Qing dynasty (1644–1912). Textiles and ceramics were the source of the cherry blossom, chrysanthemums and peonies. I made up the bell-pull in the same way as the Metallic Flower Bell-pull (see page 28).

Design size	14.5 x 88.4cm (5⁷⁄₁₀ x 34⁹⁄₁₀in)
Stitch count	80 x 487
Fabric count	14 holes per inch
Number of strands	2

Thread required

	Anchor Stranded Cotton	Amount
	1	887.7cm (349‰in)
	403	6cm (2‰in)
	337	111.6cm (43‰in)
	338	356.6cm (140‰in)
	340	520.5cm (204‰in)
	341	211.2cm (83⅓in)
	390	230.6cm (90‰in)
	337/White**	198.7cm (78‰in)
	842	45.8cm (18in)
	843	792.3cm (311‰in)
	843/845**	40.3cm (15.9in)
	845	784.4cm (308‰in)
	333	27.8cm (10‰in)
	333/905**	18.5cm (7⅜in)
	1086	335.3cm (132in)
	46	41.2cm (16‰in)
	333/46**	32cm (12‰in)
	903	437.6cm (172‰in)
	6	39.4cm (15‰in)
	8	141.2cm (55‰in)
	9	129.2cm (50‰in)
	10	105.6cm (41‰in)
	970	119.5cm (47in)
	972	320.9cm (126‰in)
	970/White**	168.1cm (66‰in)
	Black/1086**	33.8cm (13‰in)
	842/843**	62.5cm (24‰in)
	846	367.2cm (144‰in)
	178	75.5cm (29‰in)
	177	132.9cm (52‰in)
	176	171.3cm (67‰in)
	120	86.1cm (33‰in)
	36	254.7cm (100‰in)
	39	81cm (31‰in)
	36/39	150cm (59‰in)
	120/White**	53.3cm (21in)
	36/White**	192.6cm (75‰in)
	338/340**	105.6cm (41‰in)
	903/1086**	20.4cm (8in)
	403* (Claws & beak)	2.9cm (1‰in)
	903* (Thorns)	1.8cm (‰in)
	177* (Breast of bird 2)	9cm (3‰in)
	1* (Eye spot)	0.4cm (‰in)

*Back stitch   **Use 1 strand of each

A black and white version of this chart, which can be enlarged on a photocopier for easier working, can be found on pages 161–2

Bookmarks

Each of these has been worked on a ready-made bookmark from Framecraft Miniatures. I like them because, once the stitching is complete, they only need a quick press to be finished, unless, of course, you wish to add a backing.

DRAGON

This is a bright and cheerful bookmark which contains metallic thread so that the dragon's head shines.

Design size	5.2 x 21.4cm (2¹⁄₁₀ x 8⁷⁄₁₀in)
Stitch count	30 x 118
Fabric count	14 holes per inch
Number of strands	2

Thread required

	Anchor Stranded Cotton	Amount
⬛	403	77.3cm (30⁴⁄₁₀in)
	386 Perle	30.1cm (11⁸⁄₁₀in)
⬛	245	197.7cm (77⁴⁄₁₀in)
⬛	246	123.6cm (48⁷⁄₁₀in)
▨	278	75.5cm (29⁷⁄₁₀in)
▨	Gold Lamé 303††	116.2cm (45⁸⁄₁₀in)
⬛	334	39.8cm (15⁷⁄₁₀in)
	1	8.3cm (3³⁄₁₀in)
▨	266	171.3cm (67⁶⁄₁₀in)
▨	266/245†	103.3cm (40⁷⁄₁₀in)
⬛	403*	9.1cm (3⁶⁄₁₀in)

*Back stitch   †1 strand of each   ††Use 4 strands

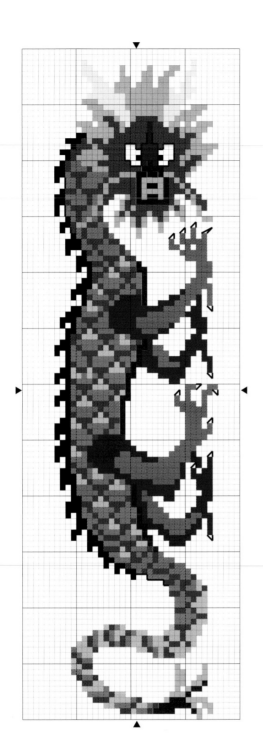

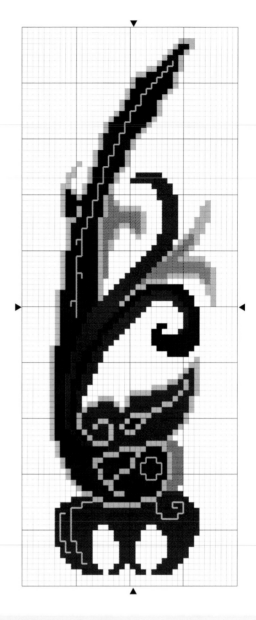

Thread required

	Anchor Stranded Cotton	Amount
	46	77.3cm (30‰in)
	298 Lamé 303†	30.1cm (11‰in)
	266	197.7cm (77‰in)
	150	123.6cm (48‰in)
	298* Lamé 303†	75.5cm (29‰in)

*Back stitch †Use 4 strands

ENAMEL BIRD

This bird design, which came from a *cloisonné* enamelled vase, was probably originally based on a phoenix. Like the above bookmark, it contains gold thread but in this case, the gold represents the gilding on the vase.

Design size	5.6 x 17.4cm (2‰ x 6‰in)
Stitch count	31 x 96
Fabric count	14 holes per inch
Number of strands	2

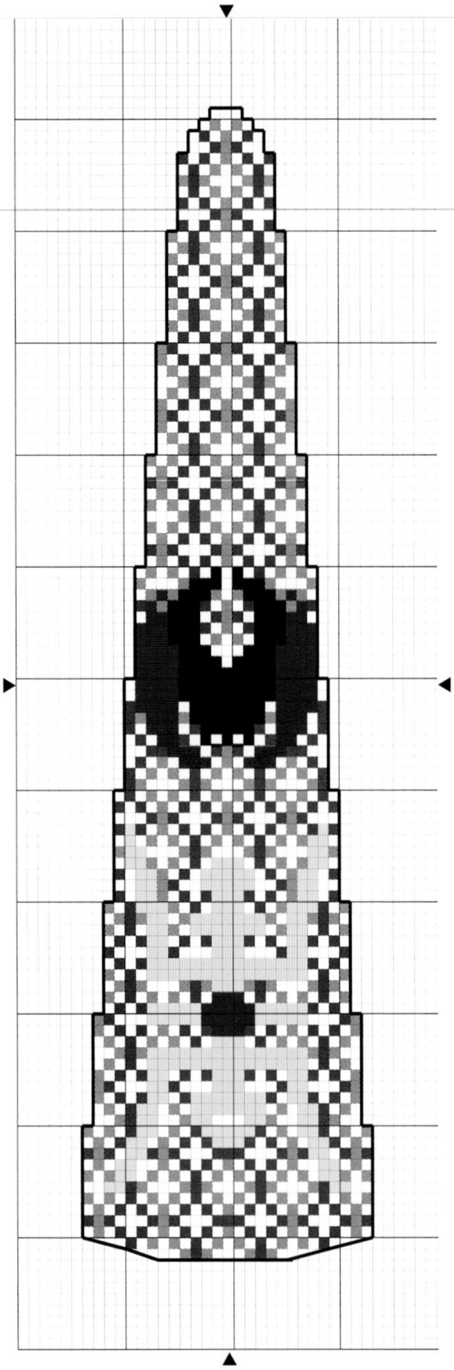

Nail protector

Chinese ladies thought long nails were a symbol of beauty, so they protected them with finely woven gilt metal and silver sheaths similar, I suppose, to thimbles. Although the protector looks large on the bookmark, it would only be a few centimetres (an inch or two) long. This nail protector is decorated with a bat for good fortune and a 'shou' sign as a blessing for long life.

Thread required

	Anchor Stranded Cotton	Amount
	403	2.8cm (1 1/10in)
	398	151.4cm (59 4/10in)
	400	160.2cm (63 1/10in)
	22	44.0cm (17 3/10in)
	298 Lamé 303†	114.8cm (45 2/10in)
	47	51.9cm (20 4/10in)
	403*	31.3cm (12 3/10in)

*Back stitch †Use 4 strands

Design size	4.9 x 18.7cm (1 9/10 x 7 4/10in)
Stitch count	27 x 103
Fabric count	14 holes per inch
Number of strands	2

Shadow Puppet Pictures

These two designs were taken from shadow puppets, which are thought to have originated in China during the Han dynasty (206BC–AD220). Chinese shadow puppets may look quite delicate, but they were usually made from treated donkey skin. This is tough and will stand a lot of handling but, when treated, it becomes translucent.

Shadow theatre is performed in China to this day and new plays are still written and new puppets specially made.

Thread required

	Anchor Stranded Cotton	Amount
▮	403	576.5cm (227in)
▮	403*	2.9cm (1¹⁄₁₀in)

*Back stitch

Design size	10.9 x 11.4cm (4³⁄₁₀ x 4⁵⁄₁₀in)
Stitch count	60 x 63
Fabric count	14 holes per inch
Number of strands	2

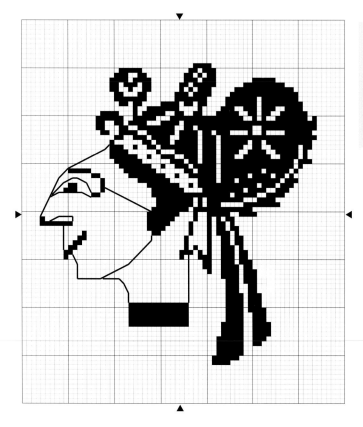

Thread required

	Anchor Stranded Cotton	Amount
▮	403	658.9cm (259⁵⁄₁₀in)
▮	403*	7.4cm (2⁹⁄₁₀in)

*Back stitch

Design size	9.8 x 11.8cm (3⁹⁄₁₀ x 4⁶⁄₁₀in)
Stitch count	54 x 65
Fabric count	14 holes per inch
Number of strands	2

Dinner Place Setting

This consists of a place mat, a serviette corner and three serviette rings. Any of the flowers from the chess-board (see page 75) will fit the serviette rings, so you could stitch a whole set of different ones, but keep the place mat the same to link the set together. The source of the designs was Chinese textiles from the Ming dynasty (1368–1644).

The place mat was stitched on 28-count Jobelan Light Moss, the serviette on white 28-count Jobelan and the rings on white 32-count evenweave, all being worked over two threads. I ironed Vilene on the back of the small flowers before cutting them out to stop them fraying.

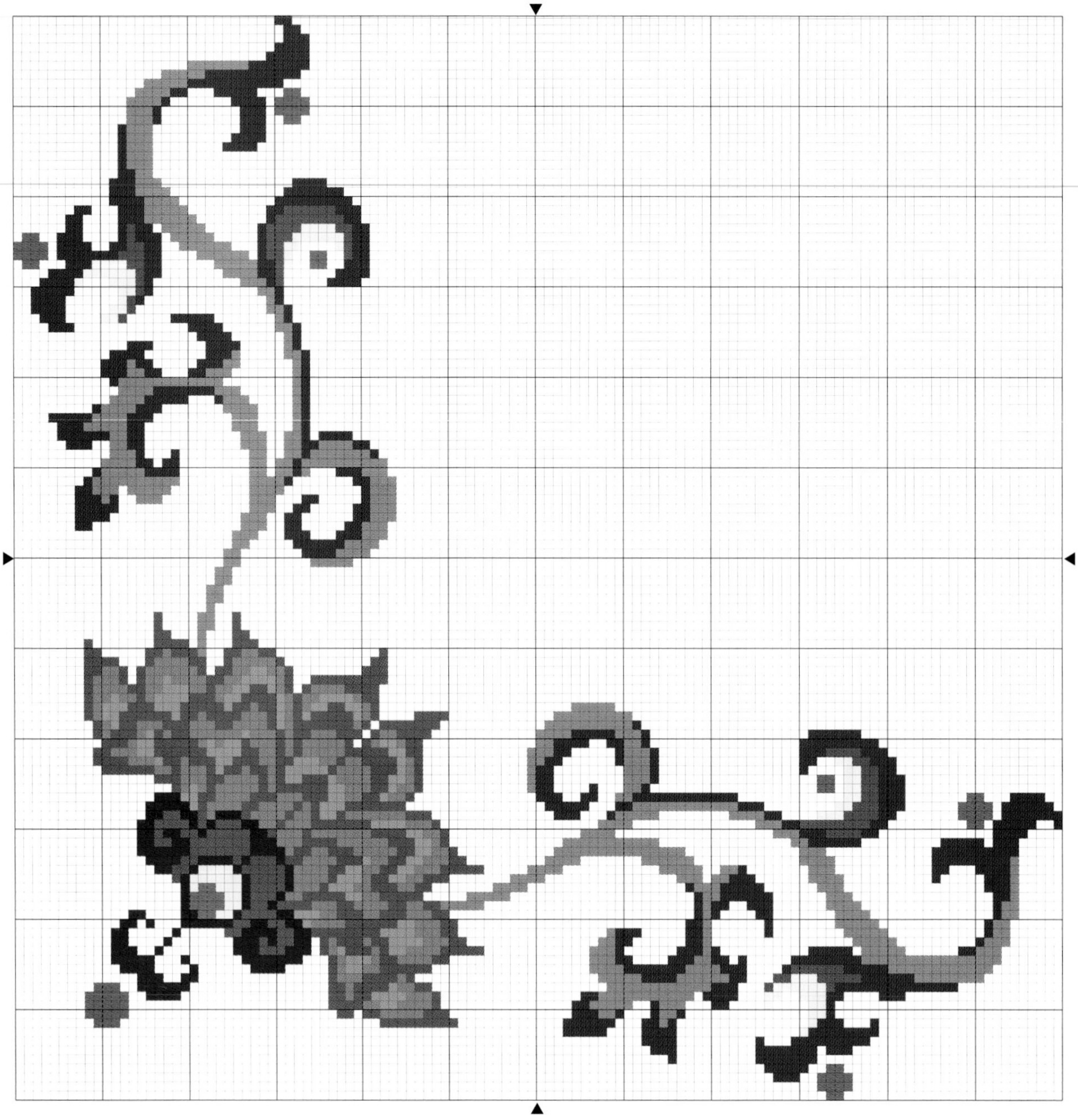

Scroll Place Mat thread required

	Anchor Stranded Cotton	Amount
	123	376.9cm (148 4/10in)
	117	320.4cm (126 2/10in)
	122	44.5cm (17 5/10in)
	386	42.6cm (16 8/10in)
	5975	258.4cm (101 7/10in)
	5975/45*	72.7cm (28 6/10in)
	337	164.8cm (64 9/10in)
	337/386*	70.4cm (27 7/10in)
	876	41.2cm (16 2/10in)

*Use 1 strand of each

Design size	21.8 x 21.8cm (8 6/10 x 8 6/10in)
Stitch count	120 x 120
Fabric count	14 holes per inch
Number of strands	2

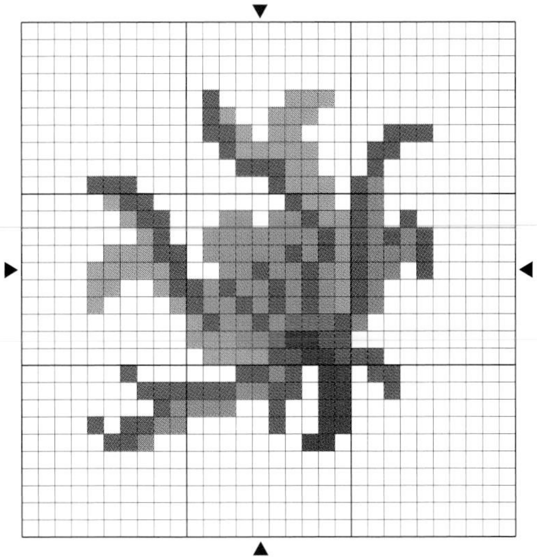

Napkin Corner thread required

Anchor Stranded Cotton	Amount
117	17.1cm (6 7/10in)
122	11.1cm (4 4/10in)
5975	29.6cm (11 7/10in)
337	10.7cm (4 2/10in)
337/386*	24.5cm (9 7/10in)
876	1.9cm (7/10in)
878	6.5cm (2 6/10in)

*Use 1 strand of each

Design size	3.8 x 3.8cm (1½ x 1½in)
Stitch count	21 x 21
Fabric count	14 holes per inch
Number of strands	2

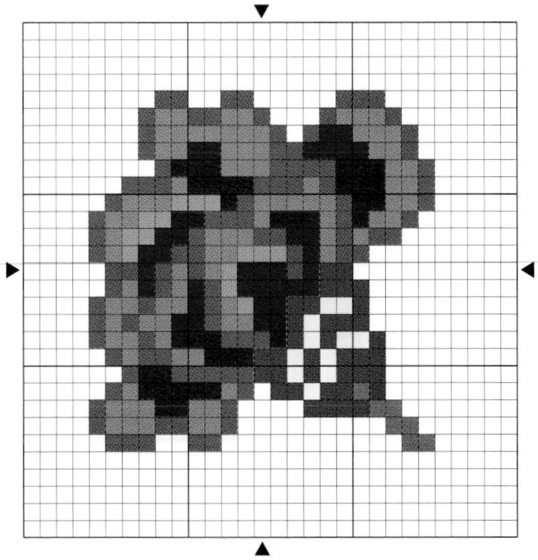

Napkin Ring 1 thread required

Anchor Stranded Cotton	Amount
386	5.1cm (2in)
5975	45.8cm (18in)
5975/45*	33.3cm (13 1/10in)
337	42.1cm (16 6/10in)
337/386*	6.5cm (2 6/10in)
876	3.2cm (1 3/10in)
878	16.7cm (6 6/10in)

*Use 1 strand of each

Design size	3.8 x 3.8cm (1 5/10 x 1 5/10in)
Stitch count	21 x 21
Fabric count	14 holes per inch
Number of strands	2

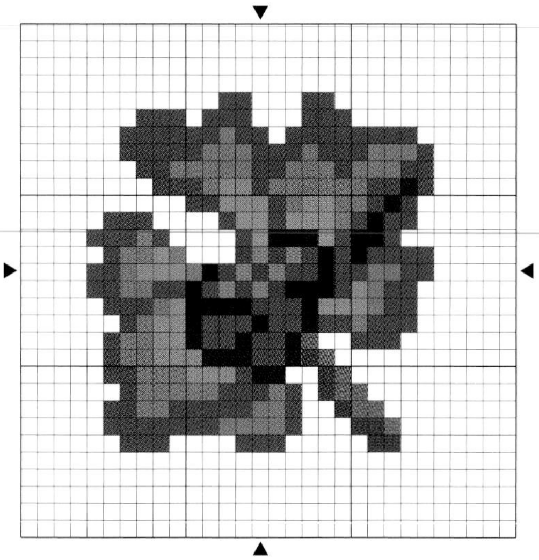

Napkin Ring 2 thread required

	Anchor Stranded Cotton	Amount
	117	2.8cm (1 1/10in)
	122	3.2cm (1 3/10in)
	5975	72.7cm (28 6/10in)
	5975/45*	15.3cm (6in)
	337	30.6cm (12in)
	337/386*	15.3cm (6.in)
	876	3.7cm (1½in)
	878	3.7cm (1½in)

*Use 1 strand of each

Design size	3.8 x 3.8cm (1½ x 1½in)
Stitch count	21 x 21
Fabric count	14 holes per inch
Number of strands	2

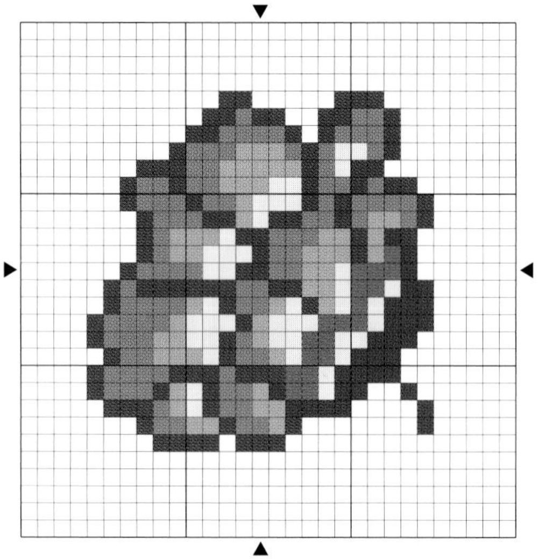

Napkin Ring 3 thread required

	Anchor Stranded Cotton	Amount
	117	43.5cm (17 1/10in)
	122	44.9cm (17 7/10in)
	386	19.4cm (7 7/10in)
	876	8.3cm (3 3/10in)
	878	14.4cm (5 7/10in)
	117/386*	23.6cm (9 3/10in)

*Use 1 strand of each

Design size	3.8 x 3.8cm (1½ x 1½in)
Stitch count	21 x 21
Fabric count	14 holes per inch
Number of strands	2

Pair of Patchwork Cushions

These designs were taken from nineteenth-century painted china vases. Stitching them, then making up the stitched flowers into patchwork cushions worked very well. The stitching on white Jobelan needs to have Vilene ironed on the back and is then treated just like any other piece of fabric used for patchwork. I think that the fabric from Marcus Brothers Textiles resembles *cloisonné* enamelling and enhances each piece of stitching to make a really stunning cushion.

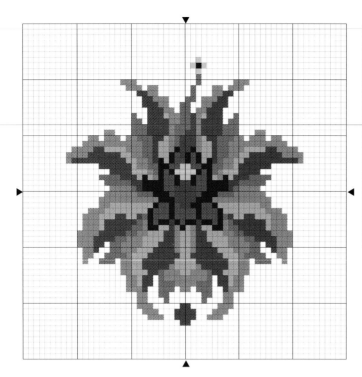

Thread required for pink design

	Anchor Stranded Cotton	Amount
	843	69.9cm ($27\frac{5}{10}$in)
	845	13.9cm ($5\frac{5}{10}$in)
	150	38cm ($14\frac{9}{10}$in)
	88	124.1cm ($48\frac{9}{10}$in)
	86	159.3cm ($62\frac{7}{10}$in)
	86/White*	77.3cm ($30\frac{4}{10}$in)
	110	24.5cm ($9\frac{7}{10}$in)
	Lamé 303†	5.6cm ($2\frac{2}{10}$in)

*Use 1 strand of each †Use 4 strands

Design size	7.8 x 8.7cm ($3\frac{1}{10}$ x $3\frac{4}{10}$in)
Stitch count	44 x 48
Fabric count	14 holes per inch
Number of strands	2

Thread required for orange design

	Anchor Stranded Cotton	Amount
	843	39.8cm ($15\frac{7}{10}$in)
	845	90.8cm ($35\frac{7}{10}$in)
	150	40.3cm ($15\frac{9}{10}$in)
	Lamé 303†	27.8cm ($10\frac{9}{10}$in)
	326	120.4cm ($47\frac{4}{10}$in)
	316	127.3cm ($50\frac{1}{10}$in)
	316/White*	59.7cm ($23\frac{5}{10}$in)
	341	66.2cm ($26\frac{1}{10}$in)
	341/White*	26.9cm ($10\frac{6}{10}$in)

†Use 4 strands *Use 1 strand of each

Design size	8.7 x 9.2cm ($3\frac{4}{10}$ x $3\frac{6}{10}$in)
Stitch count	48 x 51
Fabric count	14 holes per inch
Number of strands	2

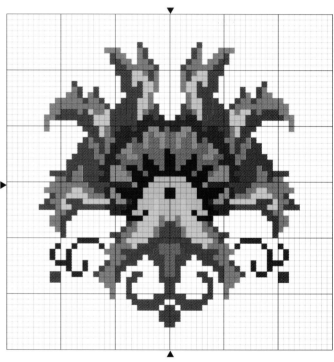

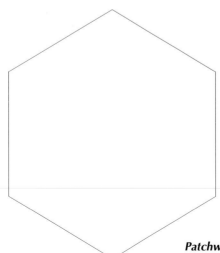

Patchwork template – photocopy to required size

Dragon Silhouette Towel Borders

These dragons were round the edge of a jade 'Bi' disk from the Zhou period (1050–221 BC). Although their exact role in Chinese life isn't fully understood, they were found in tombs, and symbolize heaven. The hole in the centre is supposed to allow lightning to flash through so that it acts as a form of protection from evil spirits for the dead.

I have used a multi-coloured thread to stitch both of these towel borders, and have shown them in two colours to demonstrate how the colouring of a design changes the character. The designs were stitched on Aida bands which can be fastened to any towel.

Thread required

1 reel Multi's Embellishment thread for each, or use 2 strands Anchor Multicolour Stranded cotton. You would need 2 skeins.

Design size	41.5 x 6.5cm (16⁴⁄₁₀ x 2⅝in)
Stitch count	229 x 36
Fabric count	14 holes per inch
Number of strands	Whole thread

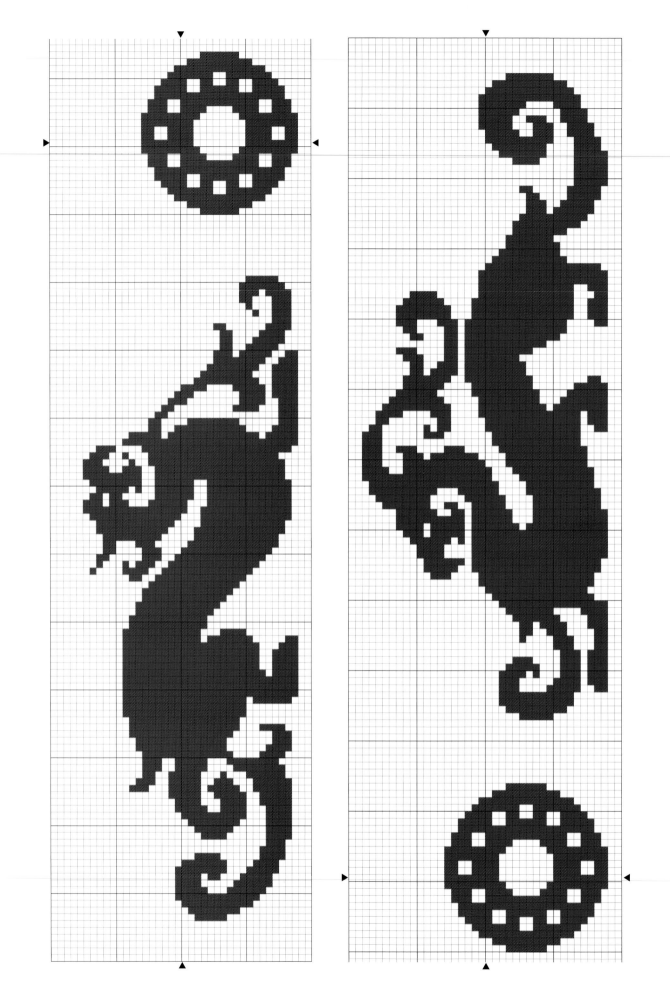

Designs from Painted Eggs

This notebook cover design and those of the two children in the frame were adapted from Chinese painted eggs. Hens' eggs were used and were polished with fine steel wool to leave a smooth, silky surface for the exquisitely delicate painting. Bright red eggs were sent out to announce the birth of a child.

NOTEBOOK COVER

The lady, carrying a dish of peaches for immortality and a wish for a long life, is shown with her flowing gown and ribbons.

Thread required

	Anchor Stranded Cotton	Amount
	403	28.3cm (11 1/10in)
	1080	43.9cm (17 3/10in)
	59	121.4cm (47 8/10in)
	939	138.2cm (54 4/10in)
	74	36.8cm (14 5/10in)
	57	321cm (91in)
	75	48.3cm (19in)
	206	90.8cm (35 7/10in)
	205	28.3cm (11 1/10in)
	205/206††	5cm (2in)
	298	28.9cm (11 4/10in)
	403*†	16.9cm (6 7/10in)
	298*†	0.5cm (2/10in)
	Mill Hill 02011**	

*Back stitch **Gold Beads †Use 1 strand ††1 strand of each

Design size	7.1 x 11.1cm (2 8/10 x 4 4/10in)
Stitch count	62 x 96
Fabric count	22 holes per inch
Number of strands	2

CHINESE
CHILDREN PLAYING

These two designs were on two separate eggs.
One is of a child holding a cymbal and beater
and the other is throwing a ball.

Chinese children were frequently shown with
these little wisps of hair tied with red ribbons. That is
because the young children had most of their hair
shaved off, leaving only the wisps; it was thought that
this helped to improve the hair growth and luxurious,
thick hair was synonymous with beauty.

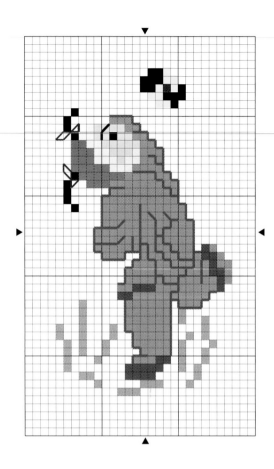

Thread required

	Anchor Stranded Cotton	Amount
■	403	10.2cm (4in)
	49	7.9cm (3⅛in)
	108	111.1cm (43⅝in)
	110	11.1cm (4⅜in)
	403/390††	10.2cm (4in)
	390/49††	7.4cm (2⅞in)
■	341	0.5cm (⅜in)
	206	19.9cm (7⅞in)
	Lamé 303†††	4.2cm (1⅝in)
■	403*†	0.2cm (⅛in)
■	46*	1.7cm (⅞in)
	110*	19.1cm (7½in)

*Back stitch †Use 1 strand ††Use 1 strand of each
†††Use 3 strands

Design size	4 x 7.4cm (1⅝ x 2⅞in)
Stitch count	23 x 41
Fabric count	14 holes per inch
Number of strands	2

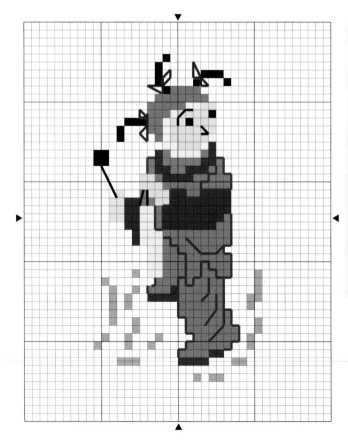

Thread required

	Anchor Stranded Cotton	Amount
■	403	9.7cm (3⅝in)
	49	19.4cm (7⅝in)
	206	16.7cm (6⅝in)
	403/390††	11.1cm (4⅜in)
	390/49††	6.5cm (2⅝in)
	337	73.6cm (29in)
	340	34.3cm (13⅝in)
	Lamé 303†††	9.3cm (3⅝in)
■	403*†	1.6cm (⅝in)
■	46*	3cm (1⅛in)
	340*	13.2cm (5⅛in)

*Back stitch †Use 1 strand ††1 strand of each †††Use 3 strands

Design size	4 x 7.4cm (1⅝ x 2⅞in)
Stitch count	22 x 41
Fabric count	14 holes per inch
Number of strands	2

Pot-pourri and Perfume Bags

These were based on designs from embroidered
and woven perfume bags from the Qing dynasty
(1644–1912). Although the designs are a matching
pair, I have stitched them in two different ways,
using different threads, to give you more ideas.

PERFUME POT-POURRI 1

This variation was worked in tent stitch on 14-
count canvas using tapestry wool and soft cotton,
then set into a firm fabric to make a cushion. I
added a twisted cord and tassel made from 8740.
You will need one skein of each colour to make
this cushion.

PERFUME POT-POURRI 2

Silk Serica, velvet ribbon and lace give a touch of
extravagance to this little bag. When complete, it
can be perfumed using aromatherapy oils, then
hung up with the ribbon tag. To make this bag
you will need two reels of 5057 and one reel of
each of the other colours.

1

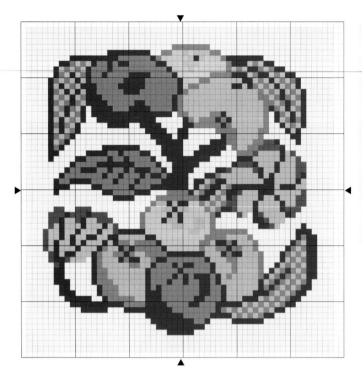

Thread required for Pot-pourri 1

	Anchor Tapestry Wool	Amount
	8740	*
	8628	*
	8624	*
	8400	*
	8502	*
	9120	*
	9382	*
	386 Soft Cotton	*

*1 skein of each

Design size	10.5 x 10.5cm (4¹⁄₁₀ x 4¹⁄₁₀in)
Stitch count	57 x 58
Fabric count	14 holes per inch
Number of strands	Whole wool

2

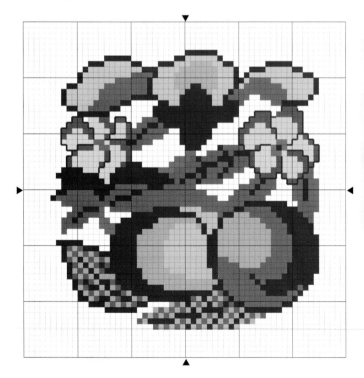

Thread required for Pot-pourri 2

	Kreinik Silk Serica	Amount
	5057	††
	5055	†
	5053	†
	1105	†
	1032	†
	4034	†
	7124	†
	5057*	†

*Back stitch   †1 reel   ††2 reels

Design size	9.2 x 9.2cm (3⁹⁄₁₀ x 3⁹⁄₁₀in)
Stitch count	50 x 50
Fabric count	14 holes per inch
Number of strands	1

Butterfly Towel

This is formed by stitching each of the three designs on 19-count Easistitch, then stitching them onto an ordinary towel. I trimmed the corners to make the overall design more interesting. Any one of the designs would make an individual card.

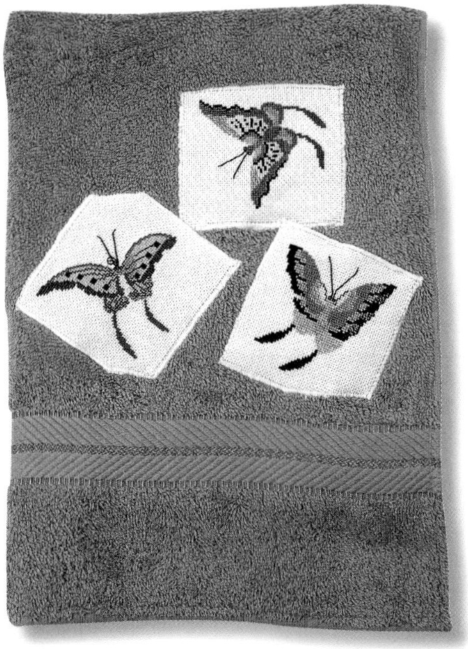

Design size	6.8 x 7.2cm ($2\frac{7}{10}$ x $2\frac{8}{10}$in)
Stitch count	51 x 54
Fabric count	19 holes per inch
Number of strands	2

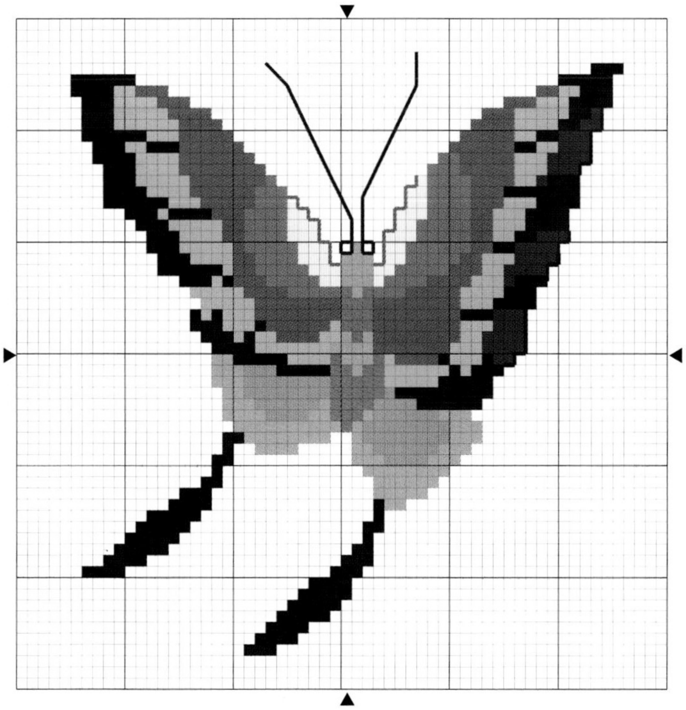

Thread required

Anchor Stranded Cotton	Amount
150	94.9cm ($37\frac{3}{10}$in)
899	12.3cm ($4\frac{8}{10}$in)
386	13.6cm ($5\frac{4}{10}$in)
874	22.5cm ($8\frac{9}{10}$in)
121/White**	59cm ($23\frac{2}{10}$in)
338	72cm ($28\frac{3}{10}$in)
338/White**	33.1cm (13in)
150/White**	16.7cm ($6\frac{6}{10}$in)
899/White**	36.5cm ($14\frac{4}{10}$in)
341*	2.5cm (1in)
150*	5.8cm ($2\frac{3}{10}$in)

*Back stitch **Use 1 strand of each

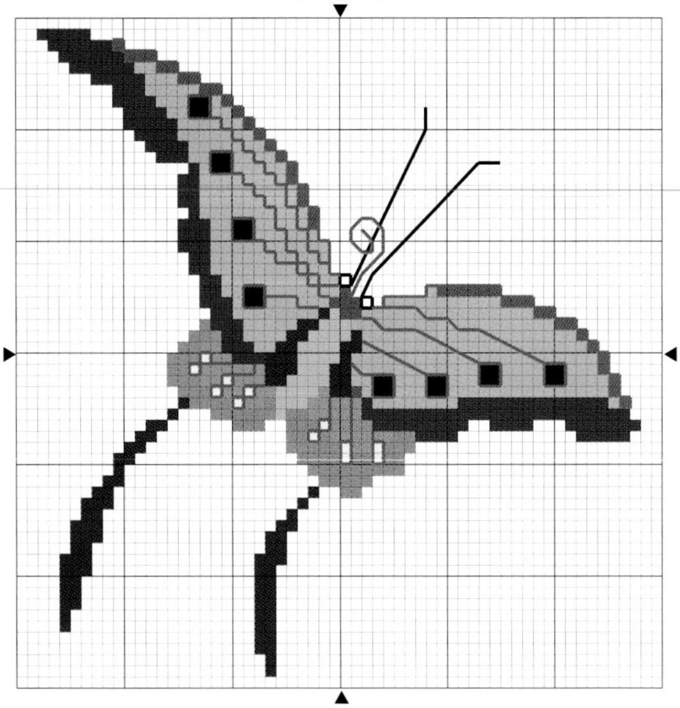

Thread required

	Anchor Stranded Cotton	Amount
	150	10.9cm (4 3/10in)
	217	56.3cm (22 2/10in)
	926	4.1cm (1 6/10in)
	338	14.3cm (5 6/10in)
	899/White**	31.4cm (12 4/10in)
	1084/899**	2.4cm (9/10in)
	341	33.1cm (13in)
	926/White**	10.6cm (4 2/10in)
	899/White**	15.4cm (6in)
	215/926**	24.6cm (9 7/10in)
	213	89.4cm (35 2/10in)
	403*	3.8cm (1 1/2in)
	341*	27.7cm (10 9/10in)

*Back stitch **Use 1 strand of each

Design size	7.4 x 7.8cm (2 9/10 x 3 1/10in)
Stitch count	56 x 58
Fabric count	19 holes per inch
Number of strands	2

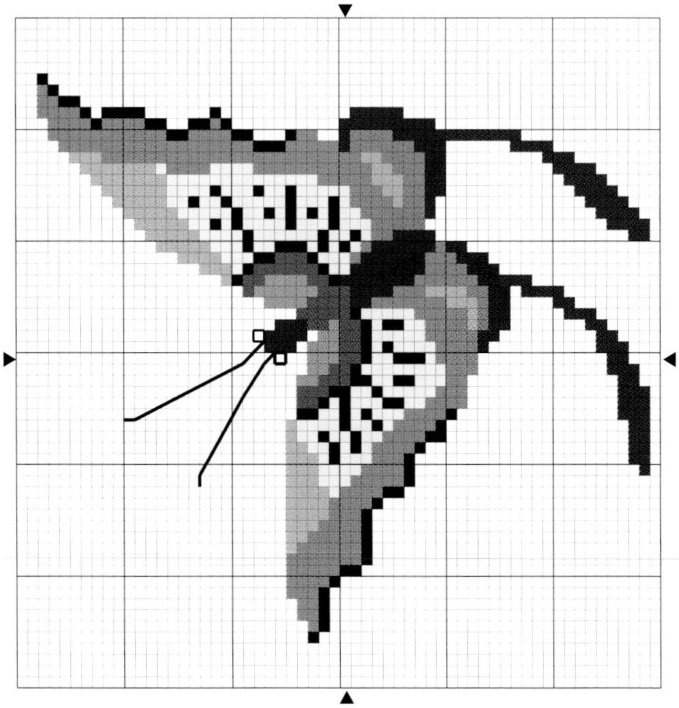

Thread required

	Anchor Stranded Cotton	Amount
	150	38.9cm (15 3/10in)
	899	17.7cm (7in)
	926	62.4cm (24 6/10in)
	874	9.2cm (3 6/10in)
	121/White**	29.7cm (11 7/10in)
	1084	34.5cm (13 6/10in)
	338	10.9cm (4 3/10in)
	121/122**	79.8cm (31 4/10in)
	899/White**	6.5cm (2 6/10in)
	1084/899**	4.8cm (1 9/10in)
	341	28.7cm (11 3/10in)
	403*	3.3cm (1 3/10in)

*Back stitch **Use 1 strand of each

Design size	7.5 x 6.8cm (3 x 2 7/10in)
Stitch count	57 x 51
Fabric count	19 holes per inch
Number of strands	2

Butterfly Cloth

I used an Afghan fabric for this and frayed the edges to make an attractive cloth which can be used either for a small table, or as a top-cloth over a dark-coloured main cloth. Any of the twelve butterflies from this cloth, the towel and the cushion centres could be interchanged, although the cloth and the towel do not contain metallic thread because of their intended use.

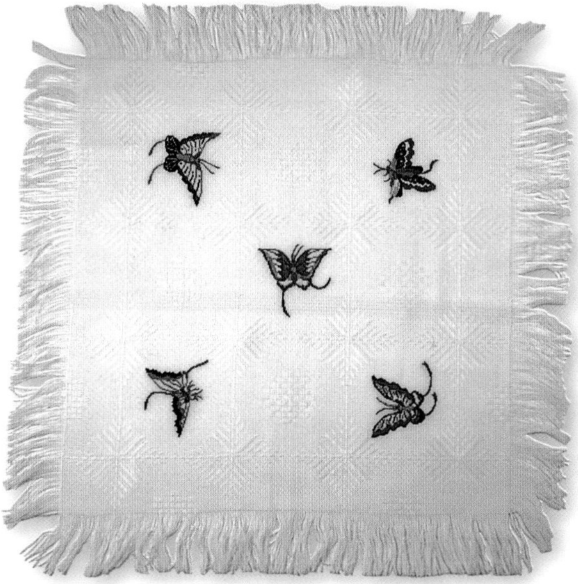

Design size	9.2 x 9.2cm (3 6/10 x 3 6/10in)
Stitch count	65 x 64
Fabric count	18 holes per inch
Number of strands	2

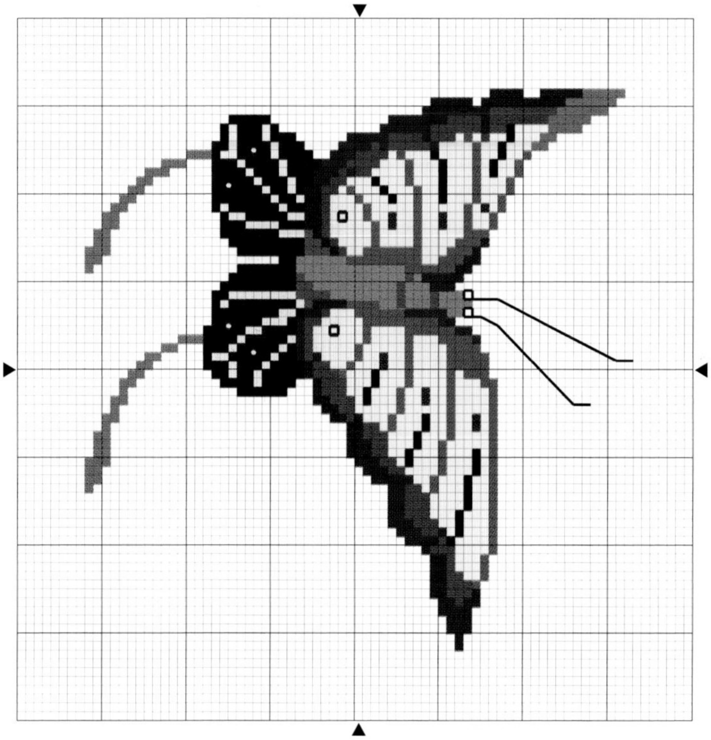

Thread required

Anchor Stranded Cotton	Amount
150	103cm (40 6/10in)
899	25.2cm (9 9/10in)
386	177.2cm (69 8/10in)
122	47.2cm (18 6/10in)
121	34.2cm (13 5/10in)
338	62.7cm (24 7/10in)
1084	7.2cm (2 8/10in)
341	12.6cm (5in)
123	63cm (24 8/10in)
403*	4.4cm (1 7/10in)
150*	0.8cm (3/10in)
386†	1.4cm (6/10in)

*Back stitch †French knot needs to be worked on each wing

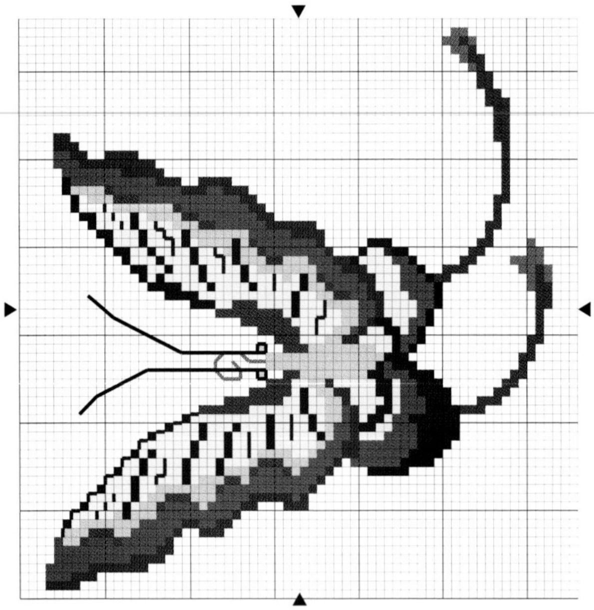

Thread required

	Anchor Stranded Cotton	Amount
	150	67cm (26 4/10in)
	386	120.7cm (47 5/10in)
	122	101.2cm (39 8/10in)
	338	7.9cm (3 1/10in)
	341	57.6cm (22 7/10in)
	123	46.8cm (18 4/10in)
	899	63cm (24 8/10in)
	403*	4.8cm (1 9/10in)
	341*	1.1cm (4/10in)
	150*	4.3cm (1 7/10in)

*Back stitch

Design size	8.5 x 9cm (3 3/10 x 3 6/10in)
Stitch count	60 x 64
Fabric count	18 holes per inch
Number of strands	2

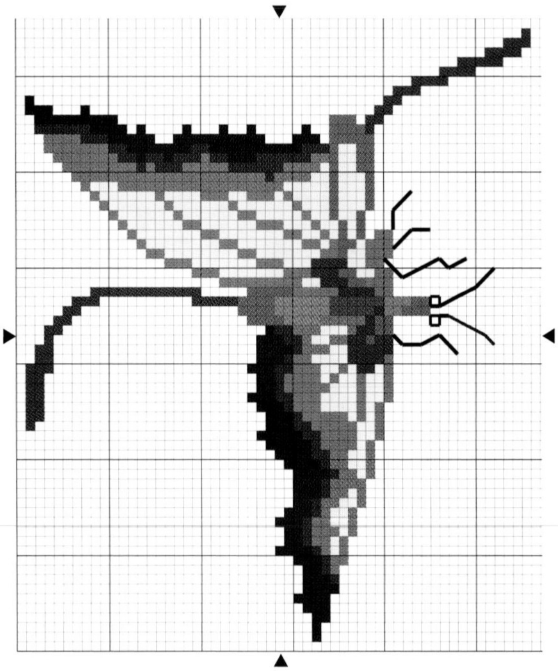

Thread required

	Anchor Stranded Cotton	Amount
	150	57.6cm (22 7/10in)
	899	7.6cm (3in)
	386	86.1cm (33 9/10in)
	122	4cm (1.6in)
	121	99cm (39.0in)
	338	24.9cm (9.8in)
	341	39.3cm (15.5in)
	123	27.4cm (10.8in)
	403*	4cm (1.6in)
	150*	0.5cm (0.2in)

*Back stitch

Design size	7.8 x 9.2cm (3 1/10 x 3 6/10in)
Stitch count	55 x 64
Fabric count	18 holes per inch
Number of strands	2

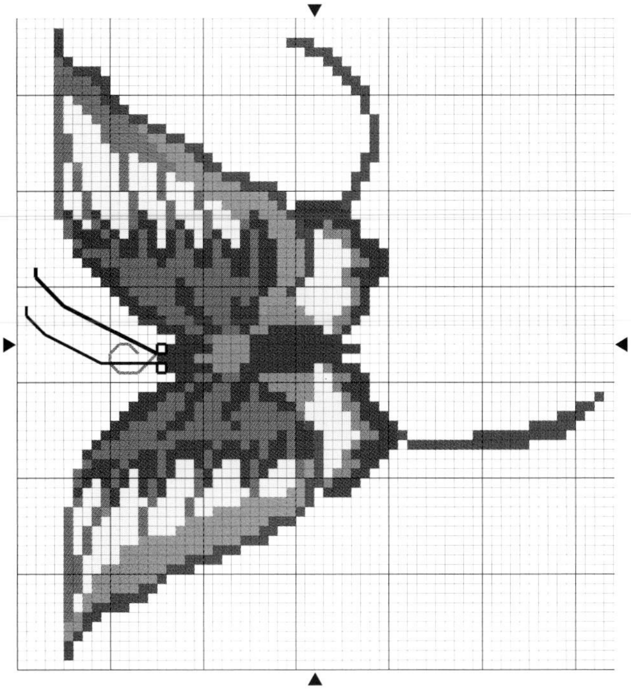

Thread required

	Anchor Stranded Cotton	Amount
	899	16.2cm (6 4/10in)
	217	56.2cm (22 1/10in)
	386	100.5cm (39 6/10in)
	1084	21.2cm (8 4/10in)
	338	101.2cm (39 8/10in)
	341	105.2cm (41 4/10in)
	215/386**	57.6cm (22 7/10in)
	215	14.4cm (5 7/10in)
	338/386**	13.7cm (5 4/10in)
	403*	3.9cm (1 5/10in)
	341†	0.9cm (4/10in)

*Back stitch **Use 1 strand of each

Design size	8.7 x 9.4cm (3 4/10 x 3 7/10in)
Stitch count	62 x 66
Fabric count	18 holes per inch
Number of strands	2

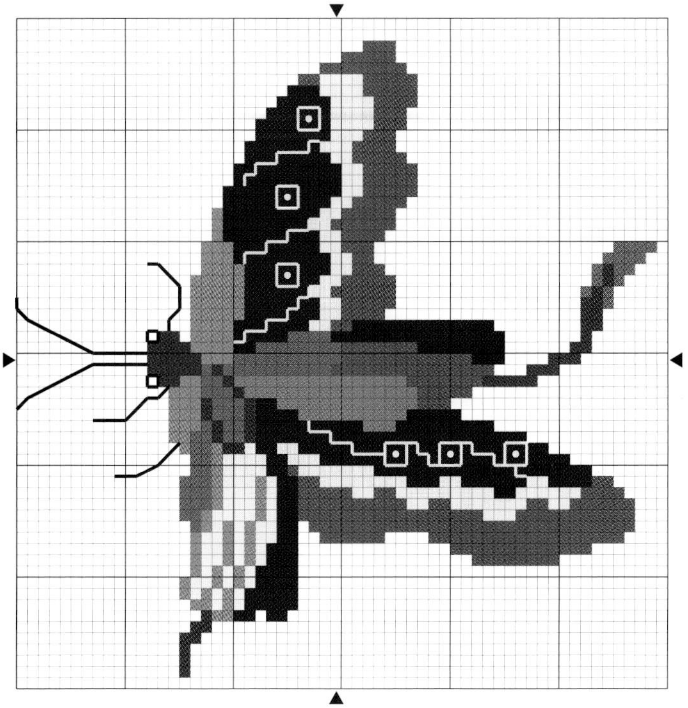

Thread required

	Anchor Stranded Cotton	Amount
	150	143.3cm (56 4/10in)
	899	36.7cm (14 5/10in)
	386	60.5cm (23 8/10in)
	122	109.1cm (43in)
	121	20.9cm (8 2/10in)
	1084	6.5cm (2 6/10in)
	338	30.6cm (12 1/10in)
	341	15.8cm (6 2/10in)
	403*	5.4cm (2 1/10in)
	386*	10.2cm (4in)
	1†	1.8cm (7/10in)
	386†	4cm (1 6/10in)

*Back stitch †French knot (6 strands)

Design size	8.5 x 8cm (3 3/10 x 3 2/10in)
Stitch count	59 x 57
Fabric count	18 holes per inch
Number of strands	2

Butterfly
Pot-pourri Cushion

Working the design

Overcast the edges to prevent fraying, then work
the design in the centre using two strands of
cotton and cross stitch.

Making up the design

Press the work well on the back using a damp
cloth. Trim the Aida to nine threads all the way
round. Stitch the embroidery in the centre of one
of the cotton squares, tack the lace or broderie
anglaise on the edge, then cover the edges with
the ribbon to make a border, allowing five threads
in excess of the stitching. With right sides facing,
stitch the back and front together, leaving a 5cm
(2in) opening to enable it to be turned through.
Trim the edges then turn the stitching the right
way out. Fill with pot-pourri or polyester, then
slip-stitch to close the opening. Attach a small
piece of ribbon as a hanging loop.

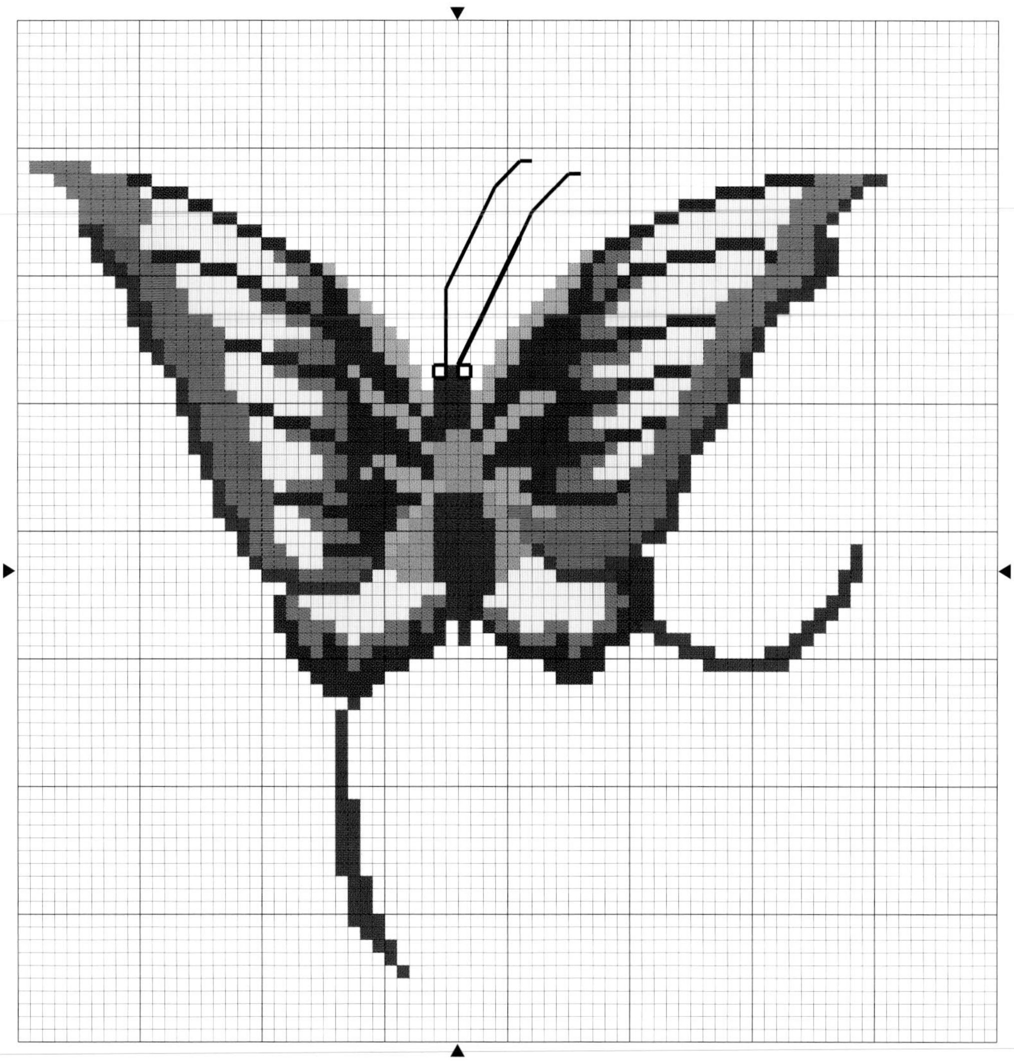

Thread required

	Anchor Stranded Cotton	Amount
	899	16.2cm (6 4/10in)
	Lamé gold 303†	33.5cm (13 2/10in)
	1084	21.2cm (8 4/10in)
	1068	59.8cm (23 5/10in)
	1066	62.3cm (24 5/10in)
	1064	31cm (12 2/10in)
	98	57.6cm (22 7/10in)
	101	129.7cm (51in)
	386	117.4cm (46 2/10in)
	403*	4.1cm (1 6/10in)

*Back stitch †Use 4 strands

Design size	9.4 x 9.8cm (3 7/10 x 3 9/10in)
Stitch count	67 x 70
Fabric count	18 holes per inch
Number of strands	2

Tissue-box Cover

I made this cover for an ordinary tissue box and it can be used for successive boxes of tissues to make them more attractive. The side edge is composed of an Aida band with the stitching, and the top is two halves of the same sort of band edged with broderie anglaise. The cover can be adapted easily to fit boxes of any size by adjusting the length of band. The design is from some fifteenth-century textiles and is the everlasting knot, one of 'The Eight Emblems of Good Fortune' which shows Buddha's mercy and gives the blessing of long life.

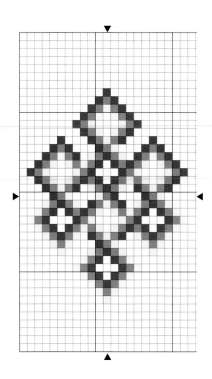

Thread required

	Anchor Stranded Cotton	Amount
	969	40.3cm (15⅞in)
	972	36.1cm (14⅕in)
	386	36.1cm (14⅕in)

Design size	3.8 x 4.9cm (1⁵⁄₁₀ x 1⁹⁄₁₀in)
Stitch count	21 x 27
Fabric count	14 holes per inch
Number of strands	2

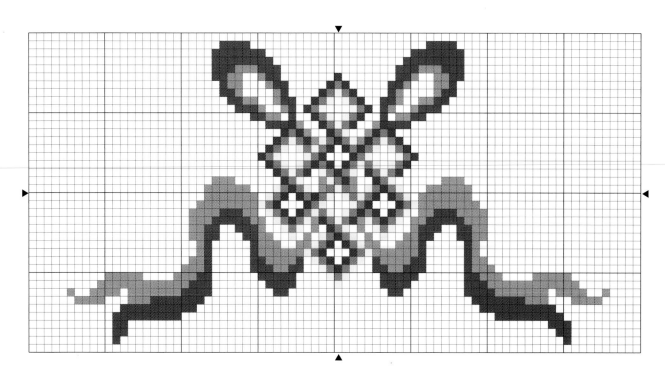

Thread required

	Anchor Stranded Cotton	Amount
	244	121.8cm (47⁹⁄₁₀in)
	240	121.3cm (47⁸⁄₁₀in)
	969	40.3cm (15⁹⁄₁₀in)
	972	35.2cm (13⁹⁄₁₀in)
	386	36.1cm (14⅕in)

Design size	12.9 x 6.8cm (5¹⁄₁₀ x 2⁷⁄₁₀in)
Stitch count	71 x 38
Fabric count	14 holes per inch
Number of strands	2

Peaches for the Kitchen

Peaches represent a wish for long life and good fortune and they occur throughout all Chinese art forms. They do not look like the peaches in western art, but have a distinctive shape and colouring. There is a commonly told story about peaches. In the royal palace gardens of Hsi Wang Mu (the Royal Lady of the West) there stood a sacred peach tree. This only gave ripe peaches once every one thousand years and anyone lucky enough to eat one of these special peaches would have immortality.

The peaches in these designs were adapted from some porcelain dishes from the Qing dynasty (1644–1912), and were painted in enamels from the *famille rose*. This is a combination of enamels, including rose pink and white, which was used for colouring the first porcelains.

CUSHION CENTRE

This was worked on 28-count Jobelan over two threads, then was set into green Jobelan NJ429.33 which exactly matches one of the greens. This linen look seems to give a rustic feel to the finished cushion which is just right for a kitchen. Combining two differently coloured threads helps to give the shaded colouring.

Thread required

	Anchor Stranded Cotton	Amount
	1014	192.2cm (75⁷⁄₁₀in)
	13/11	154.2cm (60⁷⁄₁₀in)
	11	308.7cm (121⁵⁄₁₀in)
	259	111.1cm (43⁵⁄₁₀in)
	11/259	199.1cm (78⁴⁄₁₀in)
	278	98.6cm (38⁵⁄₁₀in)
	278/259	107.4cm (42³⁄₁₀in)
	264/259	104.7cm (41²⁄₁₀in)
	878	315.8cm (124³⁄₁₀in)
	878/876	159.3cm (62⁷⁄₁₀in)
	876	262.1cm (103²⁄₁₀in)
	858	31.5cm (12⁴⁄₁₀in)
	876/858	111.6cm (43⁹⁄₁₀in)
	843/876	72.7cm (28⁶⁄₁₀in)
	1082	48.6cm (19¹⁄₁₀in)
	1082/905	122.2cm (48¹⁄₁₀in)
	403*	30.2cm (11⁹⁄₁₀in)

*Back stitch

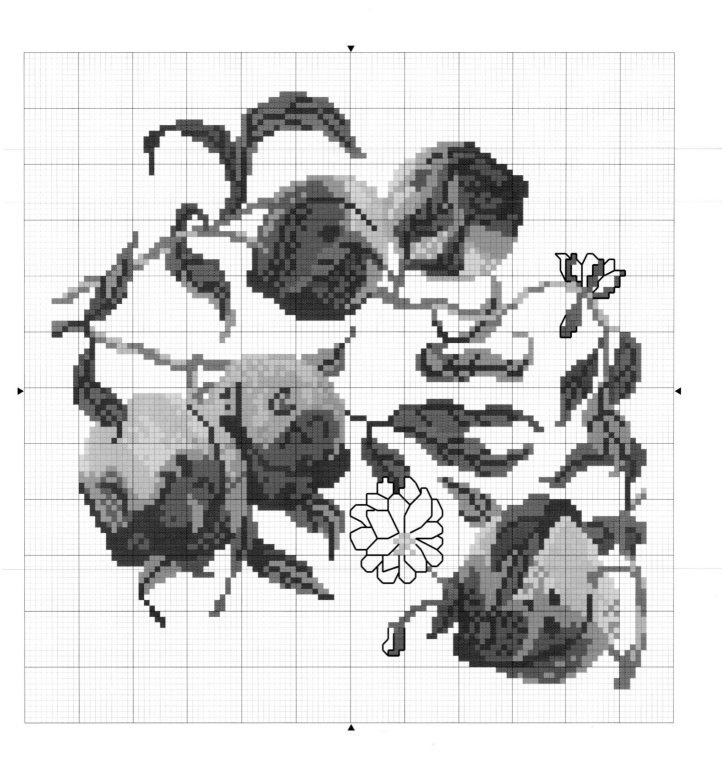

Design size	20.0 x 19.4cm (7⁹⁄₁₀ x 7⁶⁄₁₀in)
Stitch count	110 x 107
Fabric count	14 holes per inch
Number of strands	2

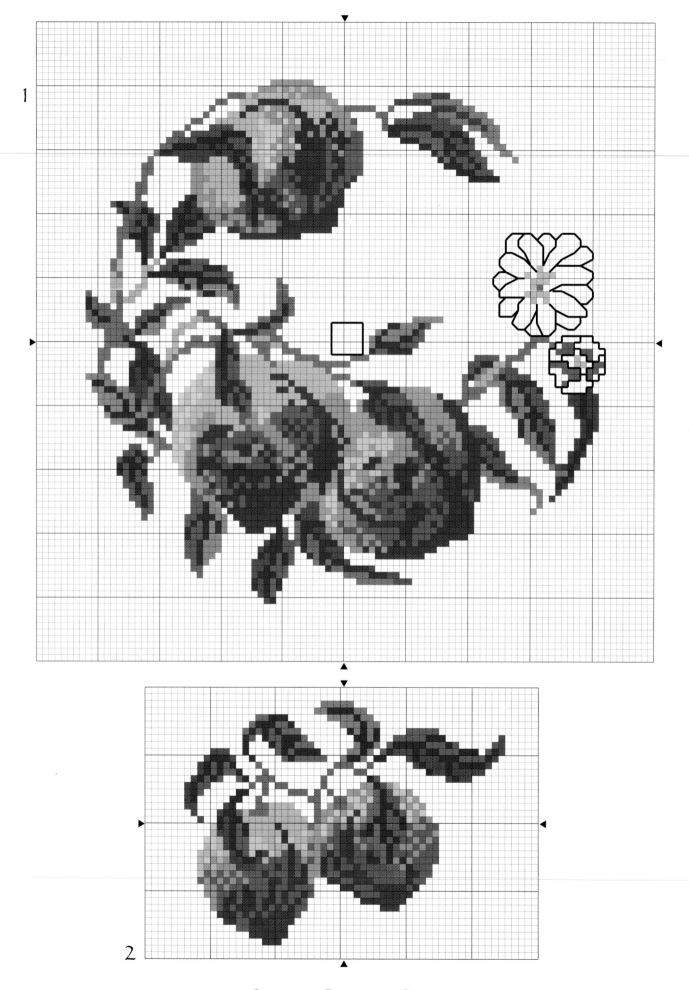

Clock

As this is a clock for a kitchen, I thought this clear, white clock ideal. The piece of 14-count vinylweave was included with the clock.

Design size	15 x 14.9cm (6 x 5 9/10in)
Stitch count	84 x 82
Fabric count	14 holes per inch
Number of strands	2

Thread required (1)

Anchor Stranded Cotton	Amount
1014/13**	134.7cm (53 1/10in)
13/11**	111.1cm (43 8/10in)
11	135.2cm (53 2/10in)
259	46.3cm (18 2/10in)
11/259**	146.3cm (57 6/10in)
278	74.6cm (29 4/10in)
278/259**	39.4cm (15 5/10in)
264/259**	32.4cm (12 8/10in)
878	188.9cm (74 4/10in)
878/876**	88.4cm (34 8/10in)
876	148.6cm (58 5/10in)
858	40.7cm (16in)
876/858**	47.2cm (18 6/10in)
843/876**	38.9cm (15 3/10in)
1082	21.3cm (8 4/10in)
1082/905**	77.8cm (30 6/10in)
403*	25.8cm (10 1/10in)

*Back stitch **Use 1 strand of each

Towel Border

This border can be repeated to any length and would make a lovely shelf border, or could be stitched along the bottom of a café curtain. I took the completed stitching with me when I bought the towel so that I could achieve the best match, and it does look quite dramatic on this dark green. It was stitched on a 75mm (3in) Aida band, then fastened to the towel.

Thread required for one repeat of the design (2)

Anchor Stranded Cotton	Amount
1014/13*	28.7cm (11 3/10in)
13/11	33.8cm (13 3/10in)
11	68.5cm (27in)
259	18.5cm (7 3/10in)
11/259*	25.5cm (10in)
278	8.3cm (3 3/10in)
278/259*	19.4cm (7 7/10in)
264/259*	10.7cm (4 2/10in)
878	62.5cm (24 6/10in)
878/876*	27.3cm (10 8/10in)
876	35.2cm (13 9/10in)
858	7.4cm (2 9/10in)
876/858*	6.5cm (2 6/10in)
843/876*	14.8cm (5 8/10in)
1082/905*	18.5cm (7 3/10in)

*Use 1 strand of each

Design size	9.0 x 6.5cm (3 5/10 x 2 6/10in)
Stitch count	49 x 36
Fabric count	14 holes per inch
Number of strands	2

Blue and White Cushion Centres

Blue and white porcelain, which came from Jingdezhen (south-eastern China), in the early fourteenth century, is synonymous with Chinese porcelain. The blues, derived from the mineral cobalt, were painted onto a white base, then covered with a clear glaze.

The following designs, which I've taken from blue and white porcelain, look dramatic when set in dark blue fabric and worked on cream Jobelan.

CARP OR MANDARIN FISH

The design for this cushion came from the centre of a dish from the Ming dynasty and shows a carp or Mandarin fish among weeds.

Thread required

	Anchor Stranded Cotton	Amount
	152	345.9cm (136⁷⁄₁₀in)
	150	608.9cm (239⁷⁄₁₀in)
	134	441.3cm (173⁷⁄₁₀in)
	147	456.6cm (179⁹⁄₁₀in)
	146	50.5cm (19⁹⁄₁₀in)
	129	128.7cm (50⁷⁄₁₀in)
	1	15.3cm (6in)
	129/White**	35.7cm (14in)
	146/147**	24.5cm (9⁷⁄₁₀in)
	150*	2.8cm (1¹⁄₁₀in)

*Back stitch   **Use 1 strand of each

Design size	18.7 x 19.2cm (7⁴⁄₁₀ x 7⁶⁄₁₀in)
Stitch count	103 x 106
Fabric count	14 holes per inch
Number of strands	2

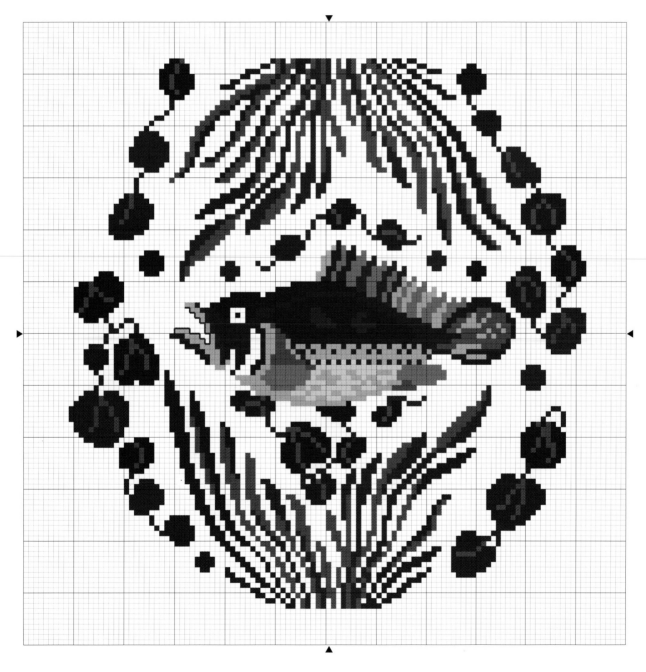

Lychees

A porcelain pilgrim's flask from the Ming dynasty was the inspiration for this design. Lychee or, in Chinese, li-chi, is a fruit grown in China.

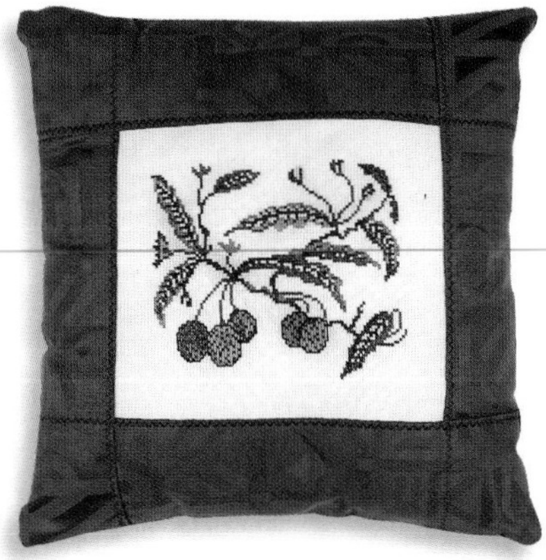

Thread required

Anchor Stranded Cotton	Amount
152	216.2cm ($85\frac{1}{10}$in)
150	284.3cm ($111\frac{9}{10}$in)
134	254.2cm ($100\frac{1}{10}$in)
147	207.9cm ($81\frac{9}{10}$in)
146	92.6cm ($36\frac{5}{10}$in)
129	25cm ($9\frac{8}{10}$in)
1	82.4cm ($32\frac{5}{10}$in)
150*†	24.3cm ($9\frac{6}{10}$in)

*Back stitch †Use 3 strands

Design size	16.5 x 13.8cm ($6\frac{5}{10}$ x $5\frac{4}{10}$in)
Stitch count	91 x 76
Fabric count	14 holes per inch
Number of strands	2

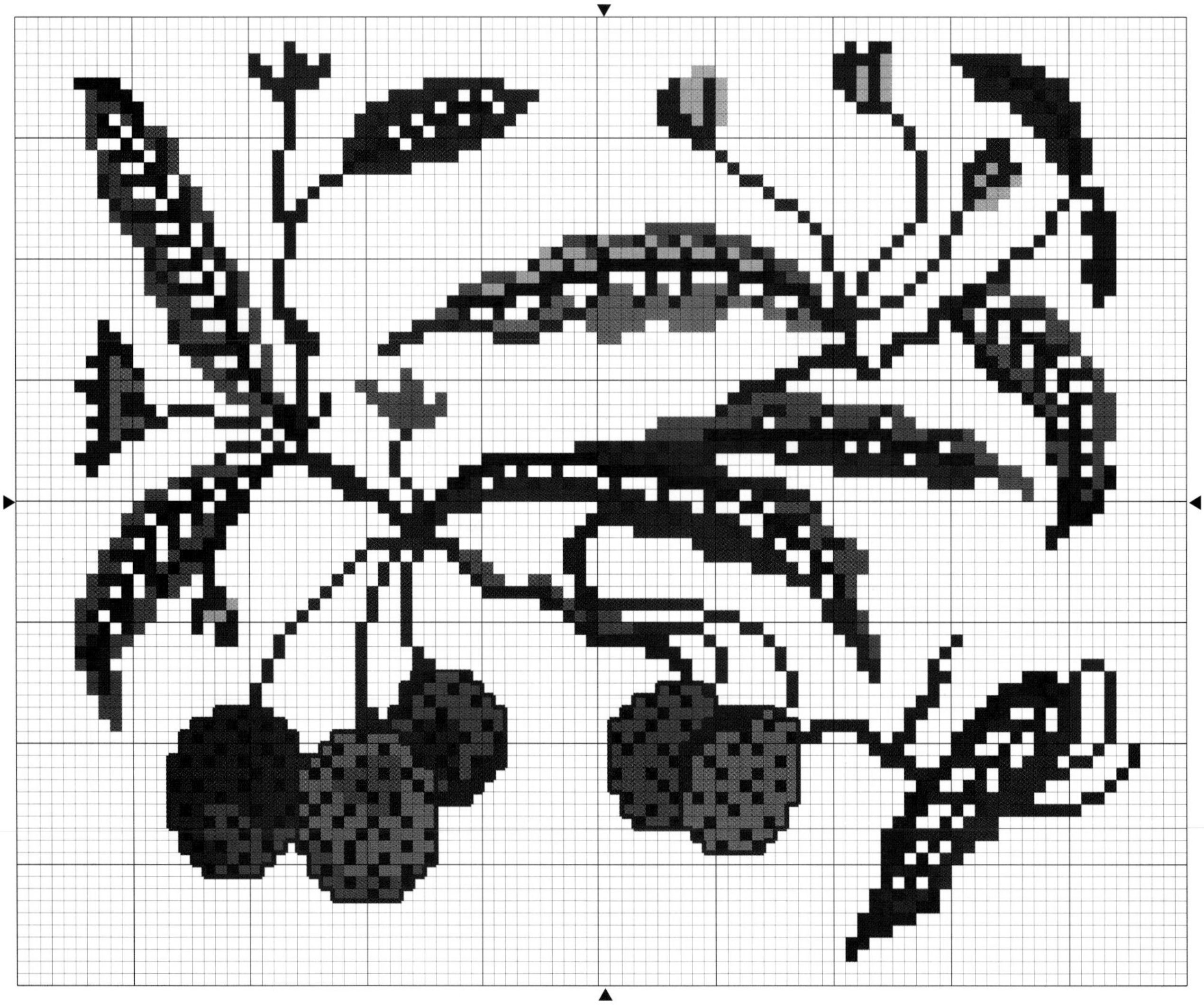

Peony

This peony, giving a blessing of wealth and honour, came from the centre of a design on a blue and white porcelain jar from the Yuan dynasty (1279–1368).

Thread required

	Anchor Stranded Cotton	Amount
	134	381.1cm (150in)
	150	167.6cm (66in)
	147	539.5cm (212⅜in)
	146	266.7cm (105in)
	129	198.7cm (78⅜in)
	152	128.7cm (50⅜in)
	147/White*	146.8cm (57⅞in)
	1	620cm (244⅛in)
	150	163.0cm (64⅜in)

*Use 1 strand of each

Design size	21.6 x 16cm (8⅝₀ x 6⅜₀in)
Stitch count	119 x 88
Fabric count	14 holes per inch
Number of strands	2

Tomb Guardian Picture

Tomb Guardian Kings, ceramic warriors complete with armour and a sword, were buried in the tombs of wealthier Chinese to ward off evil spirits. I found several pictures of these during my research and had the impression that they were quite small, so when I went to see the actual ceramic figures in the British Museum in London, I was amazed to find that some of them were over a metre (3ft) high. This particular figure has a swan at the top of its head, and would originally be gripping a weapon in the raised hand. It was standing crushing an animal under foot.

Thread required

	Anchor Stranded Cotton	Amount
	403	0.5cm (⅜₀in)
	1080	86.6cm (34¹⁄₁₀in)
	903	88.9cm (35in)
	275	138.5cm (54⅗₀in)
	326	160.2cm (63¹⁄₁₀in)
	887	160.2cm (63¹⁄₁₀in)
	843	109.3cm (43in)
	845	68.1cm (26⅘₀in)
	326/843**	122.2cm (48¹⁄₁₀in)
	884	94cm (37in)
	843/845**	73.6cm (29in)
	326/884**	55.1cm (21⅞₀in)
	887/1080**	27.8cm (10⅘₀in)
	403*	5cm (2in)

*Back stitch **Use 1 strand of each

Design size	8 x 23cm (3¹⁄₁₀ x 9in)
Stitch count	44 x 127
Fabric count	14 holes per inch
Number of strands	2

Cards from Papercut Designs

Papercuts were originally used as paper patterns for embroidery to help with repetitive patterns. Women used to cut some of them out in thick red or black paper to stick on their windows to celebrate festivals such as the Chinese New Year.

Some papercuts are very simple, but others are quite intricate and theatrical with added colour and even gold foil. I made up the two children into cards with an oval aperture of 8 x 10cm (3¼ x 4in). The green card nicely sets off the black dragon.

Design size	12.2 x 5cm (4⁹⁄₁₀ x 2in)
Stitch count	92 x 38
Fabric count	19 holes per inch
Number of strands	2

Thread required

	Anchor Stranded Cotton	Amount
■	403	455.5cm (179⅜in)

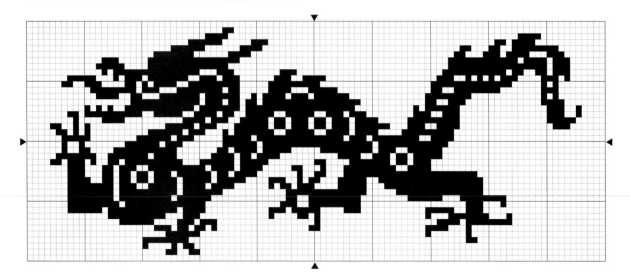

Design size	6.7 x 7.8cm (2⁹⁄₁₀ x 3¹⁄₁₀in)
Stitch count	37 x 43
Fabric count	14 holes per inch
Number of strands	2

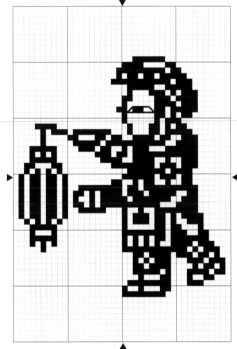

Thread required

Anchor Stranded Cotton		Amount
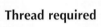	150	289.9cm (114¹⁄₁₀in)
	150*	1.1cm (⁴⁄₁₀in)

*Back stitch

Design size	6 x 6.8cm (2⁴⁄₁₀ x 2⁷⁄₁₀in)
Stitch count	38 x 43
Fabric count	16 holes per inch
Number of strands	2

Thread required

Anchor Stranded Cotton		Amount
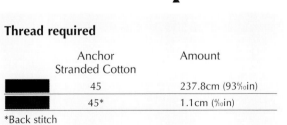	45	237.8cm (93⁶⁄₁₀in)
	45*	1.1cm (⁴⁄₁₀in)

*Back stitch

Phoenix Picture

This picture of a phoenix is an adaptation of a Qing chair cover. The original was even more detailed and had a yellow background.

Although it involved a lot of work and time, I thoroughly enjoyed stitching this design, for which I used 28-count Jobelan and worked over two threads. I am sure you will agree that the end result makes a spectacular stitched picture.

Thread required

	Anchor Stranded Cotton	Amount		Anchor Stranded Cotton	Amount
	403	0.9cm (⅜in)		390	533.4cm (210in)
	341	415.8cm (163⅞in)		390/388**	208.4cm (82in)
	339	299.1cm (117⅞in)		388	456.6cm (179⅞in)
	338	14.8cm (5⅞in)		343/388**	138cm (54⅜in)
	337	113.9cm (44⅞in)		1	212.1cm (83⅜in)
	337/White**	356.6cm (140⅞in)		878/149**	255.6cm (100⅞in)
	879	984.5cm (387⅞in)		White/390**	217.6cm (85⅞in)
	877	802.9cm (316⅛in)		1084/390**	310.2cm (122⅛in)
	875	342.7cm (134⅞in)		872	408.4cm (160⅞in)
	149	905.7cm (356⅞in)		870	308.4cm (121⅜in)
	132	660.3cm (260in)		870/White**	188.9cm (74⅜in)
	131	450.1cm (177⅜in)		403* (Eye)	2.5cm (1in)
	343	161.1cm (63⅜in)		341* (Claws)	3cm (1⅛in)
	1096	175cm (68⅞in)		872* (Flowers)	16cm (6⅜in)
	921	419.5cm (165⅜in)			

*Back stitch   **Use 1 strand of each

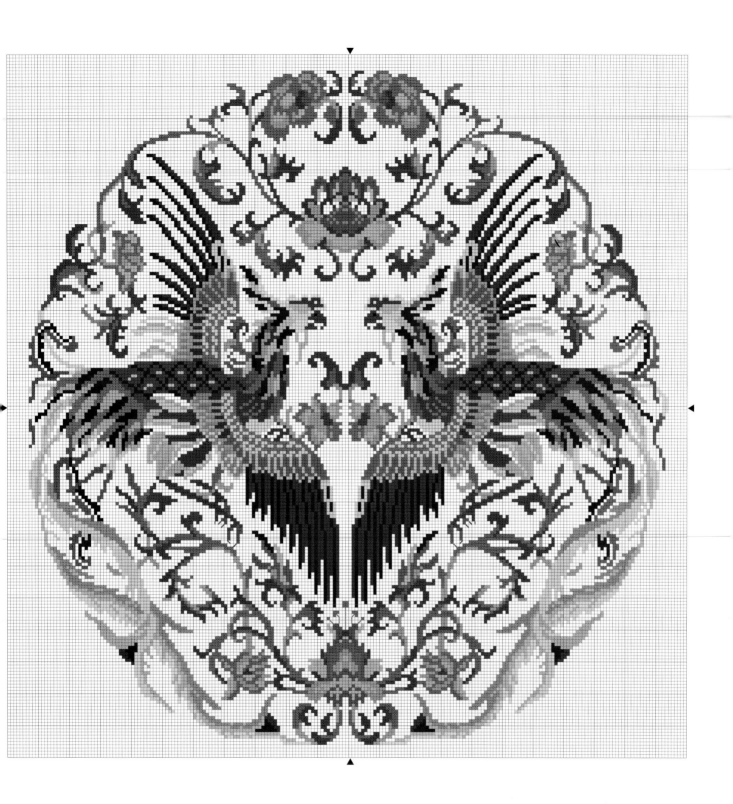

Design size	37.6 x 38.3cm (14⁹⁄₁₀ x 15¹⁄₁₀in)
Stitch count	207 x 211
Fabric count	14 holes per inch
Number of strands	2

A black and white version of this chart, which can be enlarged on a photocopier for easier working, can be found on pages 163–4

Carrier-bag Holder

The design on this useful storage bag has been adapted from some Qing stencil-printed cotton. The bag is simply a hanging tube with an elasticated bottom and the plastic bags are pushed in at the top and pulled out at the bottom.

This could be one solution to the problem of finding a present for the 'person who has everything'!

Design size	30.3 x 10.7cm (11⁹⁄₁₀ x 4²⁄₁₀in)
Stitch count	167 x 59
Fabric count	14 holes per inch
Number of strands	2

Thread required

	Anchor Stranded Cotton	Amount
	1043	103.7cm (40⁸⁄₁₀in)
	241	170.4cm (67¹⁄₁₀in)
	243	232.5cm (91⁵⁄₁₀in)
	245	111.6cm (43⁹⁄₁₀in)
	246	326.9cm (128⁷⁄₁₀in)
	386	100cm (39in)
	145	38cm (14⁹⁄₁₀in)
	137	50.9cm (20¹⁄₁₀in)
	139	69.5cm (27³⁄₁₀in)
	149	217.6cm (85⁷⁄₁₀in)
	Lame 303†	74.1cm (29²⁄₁₀in)

†Use 4 strands

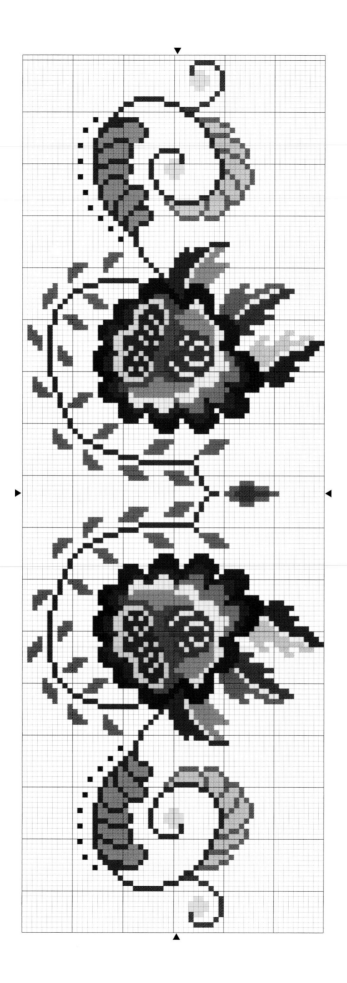

Bolster Cushion Borders

These three border designs originated from an enamelled bottle and could be useful for a variety of purposes.

Thread required

	Anchor Stranded Cotton	Amount
	1036	25cm (9⅞in)
	1	22.2cm (8⅞in)
	59	5.6cm (2⅖in)
	1002	23.2cm (9¹⁄₁₀in)
	266	113cm (44⅝in)

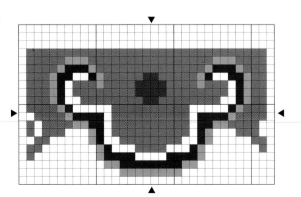

Design size	5.6 x 2.7cm (2²⁄₁₀ x 1¹⁄₁₀in)
Stitch count	31 x 16
Fabric count	14 holes per inch
Number of strands	2

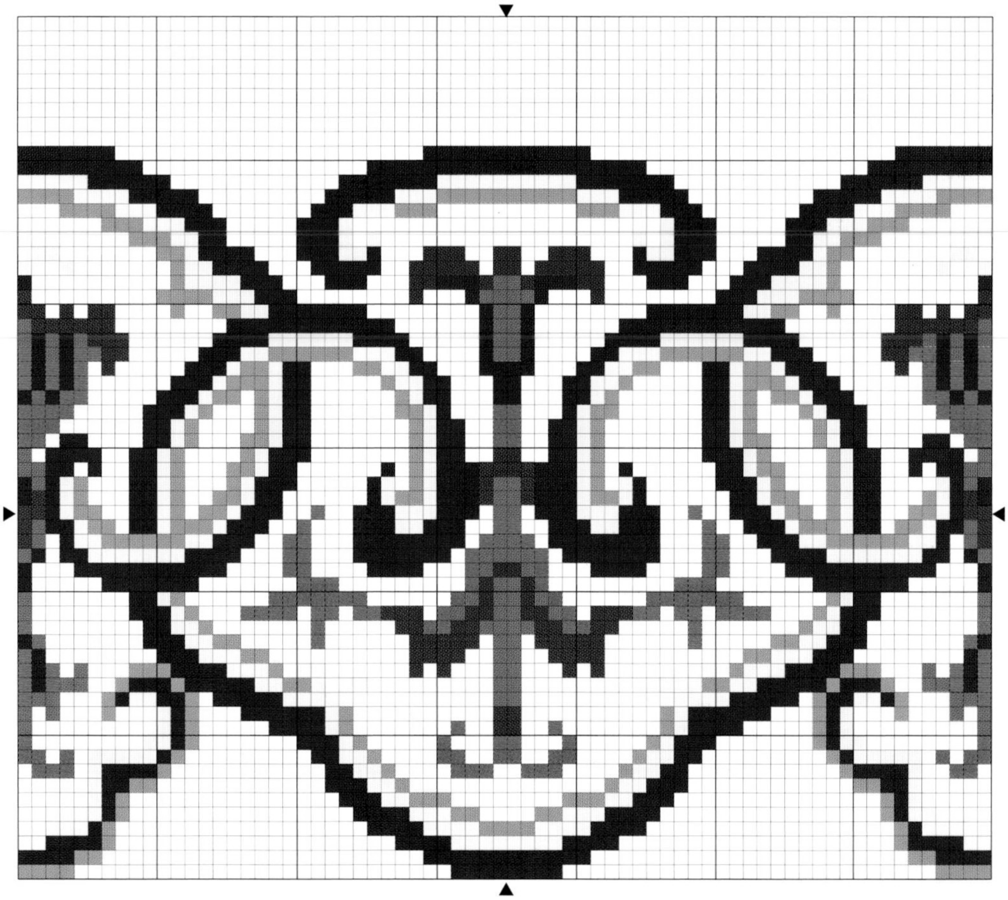

Thread required

	Anchor Stranded Cotton	Amount
	1036	385.3cm (151$\frac{7}{10}$in)
	1	171.3cm (67$\frac{5}{10}$in)
	59	62cm (24$\frac{4}{10}$in)
	1002	132cm (52in)
	59/White*	44.5cm (17$\frac{5}{10}$in)
	266	78.3cm (30$\frac{8}{10}$in)

*Use 1 strand of each

Design size	12.7 x 9.2cm (5 x 3$\frac{6}{10}$in)
Stitch count	70 x 51
Fabric count	14 holes per inch
Number of strands	2

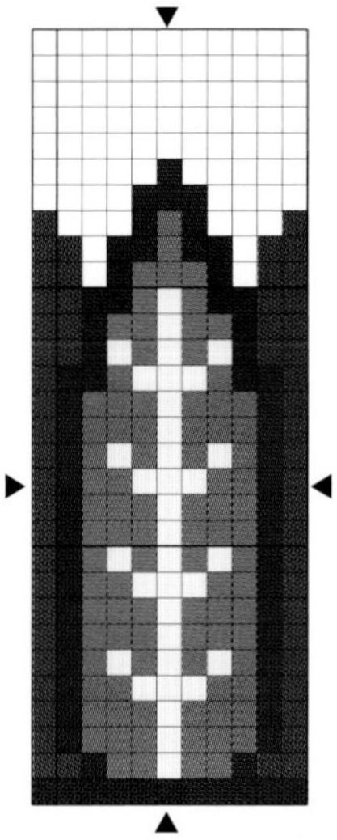

Thread required

	Anchor Stranded Cotton	Amount
	1036	29.6cm (11$\frac{7}{10}$in)
	1	16.2cm (6$\frac{4}{10}$in)
	59	15.7cm (6$\frac{2}{10}$in)
	266	42.1cm (16$\frac{6}{10}$in)

Design size	1.8 x 4.5cm ($\frac{7}{10}$ x 1$\frac{8}{10}$in)
Stitch count	10 x 25
Fabric count	14 holes per inch
Number of strands	2

Towel Border

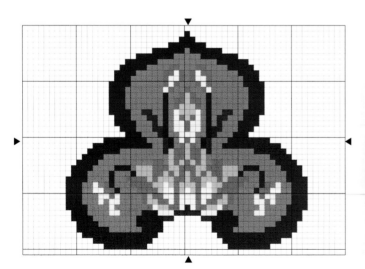

Design size	8 x 7.1cm (3²/₁₀ x 2⁸/₁₀in)
Stitch count	45 x 39
Fabric count	14 holes per inch
Number of strands	2

This repetitive design was adapted from a small section of a painted china jar. It was worked on a 75mm (3in) Aida border, then stitched to the towel.

Thread required

	Anchor Stranded Cotton	Amount
	218	198.7cm (78²/₁₀in)
	217	14.8cm (5⁸/₁₀in)
	214	196.8cm (77⁵/₁₀in)
	10	61.1cm (24¹/₁₀in)
	8	33.8cm (13³/₁₀in)
	386	37cm (14⁶/₁₀in)

Mandarin Duck Card

Mandarin ducks are regarded by the Chinese in a similar way to that in which we regard white heather, horseshoes and black cats. They are a symbol of good luck and fidelity and are often found in marriage wishes.

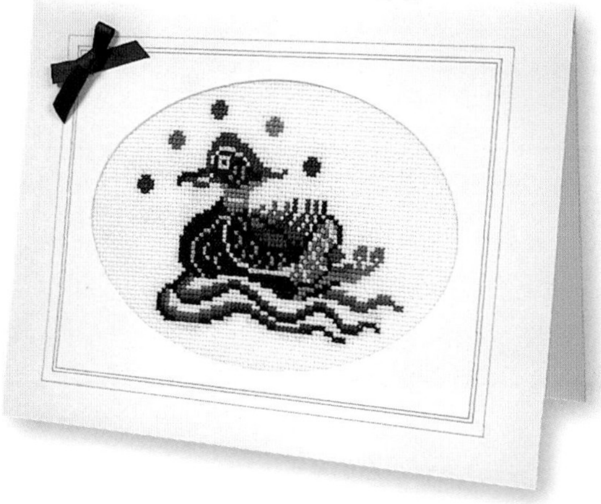

Thread required

Colour	Anchor Stranded Cotton	Amount
	152	204.2cm (80 4/10in)
	147	100.5cm (39 6/10in)
	149	17.8cm (7in)
	146	62.8cm (24 7/10in)
	145	40.5cm (16in)
	128	17cm (6 7/10in)
	386	30.8cm (12 1/10in)

Design size	10.5 x 7.8cm (4 1/10 x 3 1/10in)
Stitch count	66 x 50
Fabric count	16 holes per inch
Number of strands	2

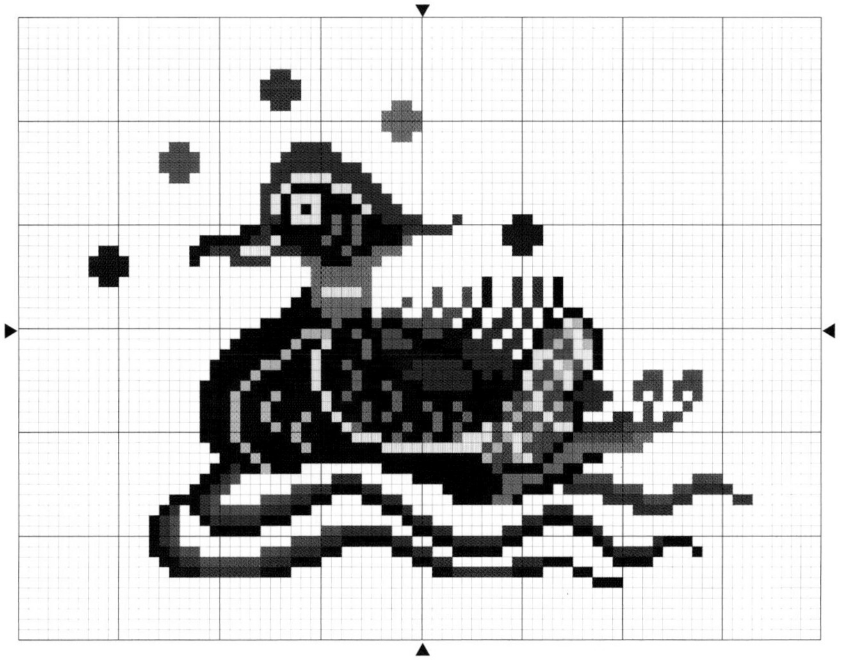

Wooden Box and Card

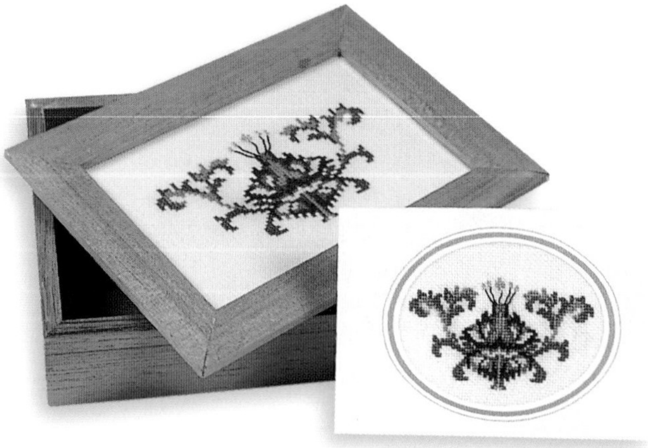

This design was adapted from the centre of a nineteenth-century painted china dish.

Design size	12.2 x 7.1cm (4 8/10 x 2 8/10in)
Stitch count	67 x 39
Fabric count	14 holes per inch
Number of strands	2

Thread required

	Anchor Stranded Cotton	Amount
	217	160.7cm (63 3/10in)
	215	75.0cm (29 5/10in)
	386	34.3cm (13 5/10in)
	338	41.2cm (16 2/10in)
	341	86.6cm (34 1/10in)
	Lamé 303†	7.4cm (2 9/10in)
	403*	3.5cm (1 4/10in)

*Back stitch †Use 4 strands

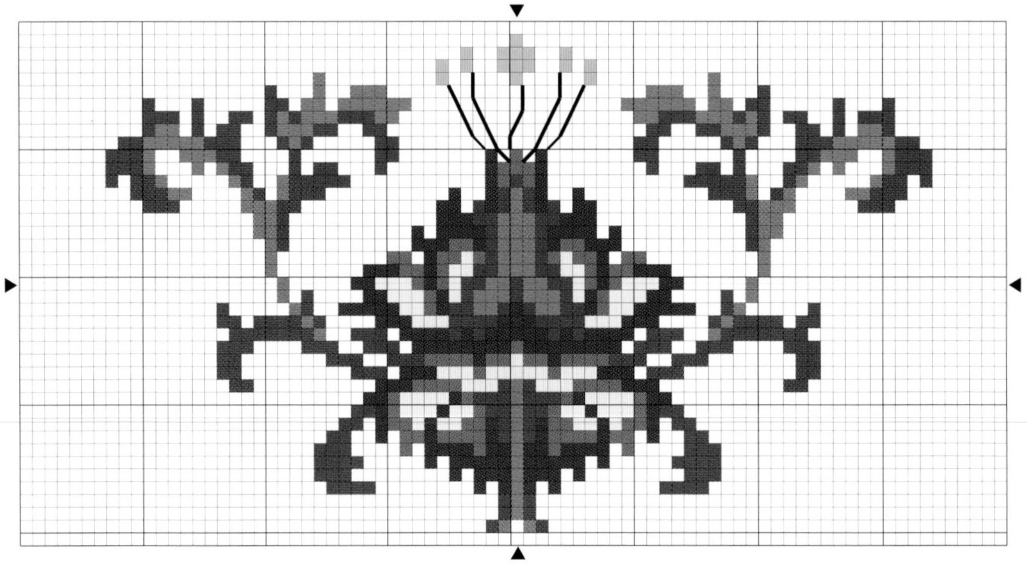

Thread Conversion Chart

This conversion chart is for guidance only, as exact comparisons are not always possible.

Anchor	DMC	Madeira	Anchor	DMC	Madeira	Anchor	DMC	Madeira
1	B5200	2401	120	3747	0909	232	3042/452	1807
6	3779	2605	121	793	0906	235	318/414	1801
8	353/3824	0304	122	3807	2702	236	413/3799	1713
9	352	0303	123	820/3750	0914	240	966	1209
10	351	0406	127	1008	823	241	722	1307
11	350	0213	129	794	0907	243	948/988	1306
13	347	0211	130	794	0907	244	987	1305
19	817/304	0407	131	841/798	0911	245	701	1305
22	815	2501	134	898/820	0914	246	986	1404
36	963/3326	0503	137	798	0911	253	772	1604
38	956/3731	0611	139	797	0912	259	772	1604
39	309	0507	145	799	0910	266	470/3347	1502
43	814/498	0514	146	798	0911	275	746	0101
44	815	0513	147	797	0912	278	472	1414
45	814	2606	149	336	1006	298	972	0107
46	666	0210	150	336/823	1007	314	741	0203
47	321/304	0510	152	939	1009	316	740	0202
49	3689	0607	175	794	0907	326	720	0309
57	3805	0702	176	793	0906	333	900/608	0206
59	3350/326	0603	177	792	0905	334	606	0209
74	3716	0606	178	791	0904	335	606	0209
75	962/3733	0505	185	964	1112	336	945	2313
76	3731/961	0505	186	959	1113	339	920	0312
78	3803/600	2609	188	3812/943	2706	340	919	0313
86	3608	0709	203	817/954	1211	341	918	0314
88	718	0707	204	913	1212	343	932	1710
89	917	0706	205	911	1213	360	938/839	2005
98	553	0712	206	504/564	1210	368	436	2011
101	552/550	0713	213	304/369	1511	369	435	2010
108	210	2711	214	3817/368	2604	372	372	2110
109	209	2711	215	368/320	1310	374	420	2104
110	208	2710	216	367	1310	376	842	1910
117	341	0901	217	920	1312	378	407/841	2601
118	340	0902	218	319	1313	379	407/840	2601
119	333	0903	228	352/700	1303	386	3823/746	2512

Anchor	DMC	Madeira	Anchor	DMC	Madeira	Anchor	DMC	Madeira
388	3033	1907	882	407/3773	2312	1013	356/3778	2310
390	3033/822	1908	884	400	2305	1014	3777	2502
398	415	1802	887	3046	2206	1024	3712	0406
400	317	1714	888	370/3045	2112	1027	3722	0812
401	535/413	1713	889	869/610	2105	1028	3685	2608
403	310	2400	893	224	0404	1033	932	1710
779	3768	2508	894	3326	0813	1036	3750	1712
842	3013	1605	895	223	0812	1042	504	1701
843	3012	1606	896	3721/315	0810	1043	369	1309
845	3011	1607	897	221/902	2606	1060	3811	1111
846	936	1507	899	3023	1906	1064	597	1110
848	927	1708	903	3032	2002	1066	3809	2507
850	926	1707	904	3032	–	1068	3808	2507
851	924	1706	905	3021/3031	1904	1080	842	1910/1909
852	613	2109	921	3768/931	2508	1082	842	1910
853	435/613	2110	926	3033/712	1908	1084	841	1911
858	524	1512	939	793	0906	1086	3790	1905
870	3042	0807	943	422	2102	1089	996	1103
874	3821/834	2510	944	829/889	2113	1096	775	1001
875	504/3817	1702	968	778	0808	1098	350	0213
876	503/3816	1703	969	316	0809	5975	356	0402
877	502/3817	1205	970	3803/3726	2609			
878	501	1205	972	3803/915	2609			
879	991/500	1204	1002	977	2301			

Black and White Charts for Enlarging

These black and white charts of selected designs can be enlarged on a photocopier to make them easier to use. We recommend an enlargement of 200%.

Astrological
Wall-hanging
(see page 18)

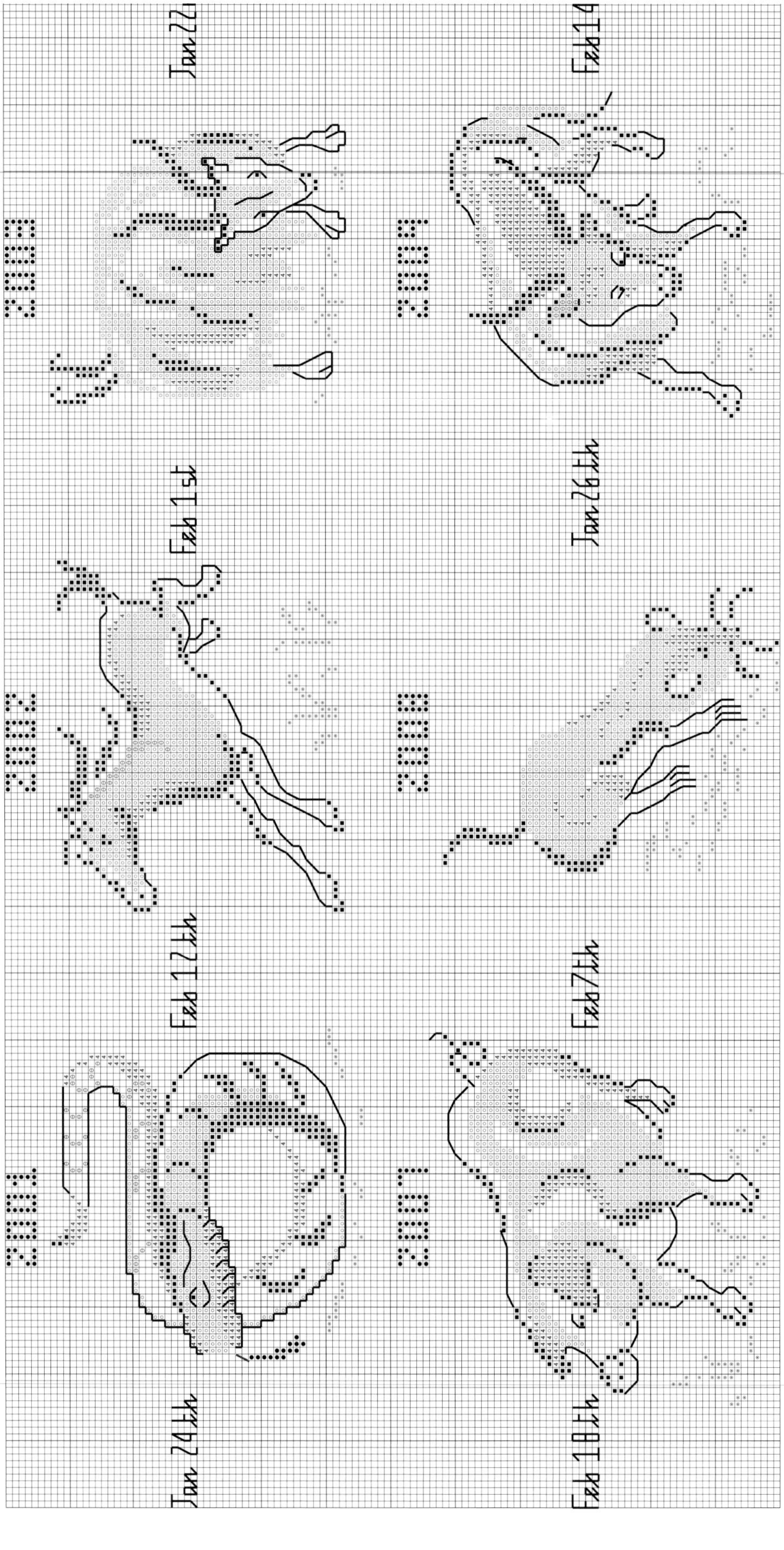

Jan 22

Feb 14

Feb 15t

Jan 26th

Feb 12th

Feb 7th

Jan 24th

Feb 18th

■ 403
○ 882
⊖ 232
● 1098
4 232/1080
◉ 266

Astrological
Wall-hanging
(see page 18)

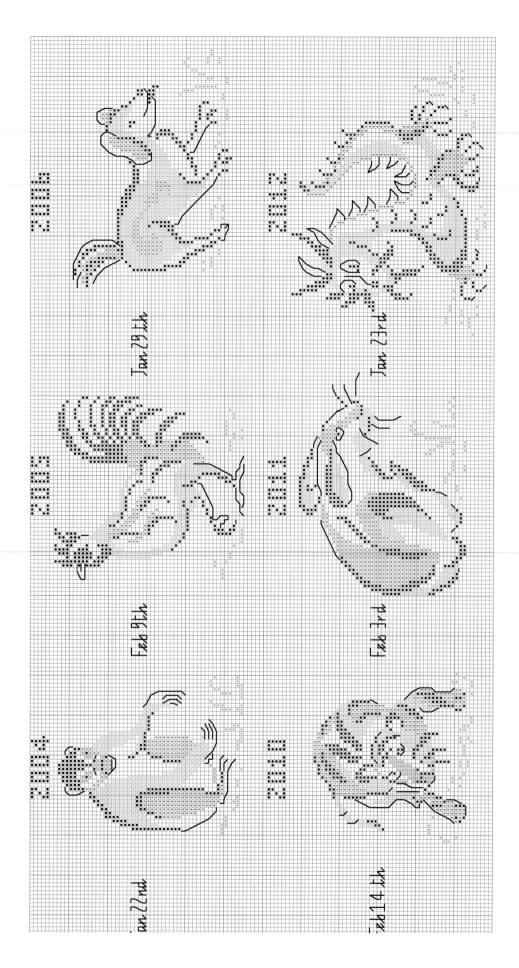

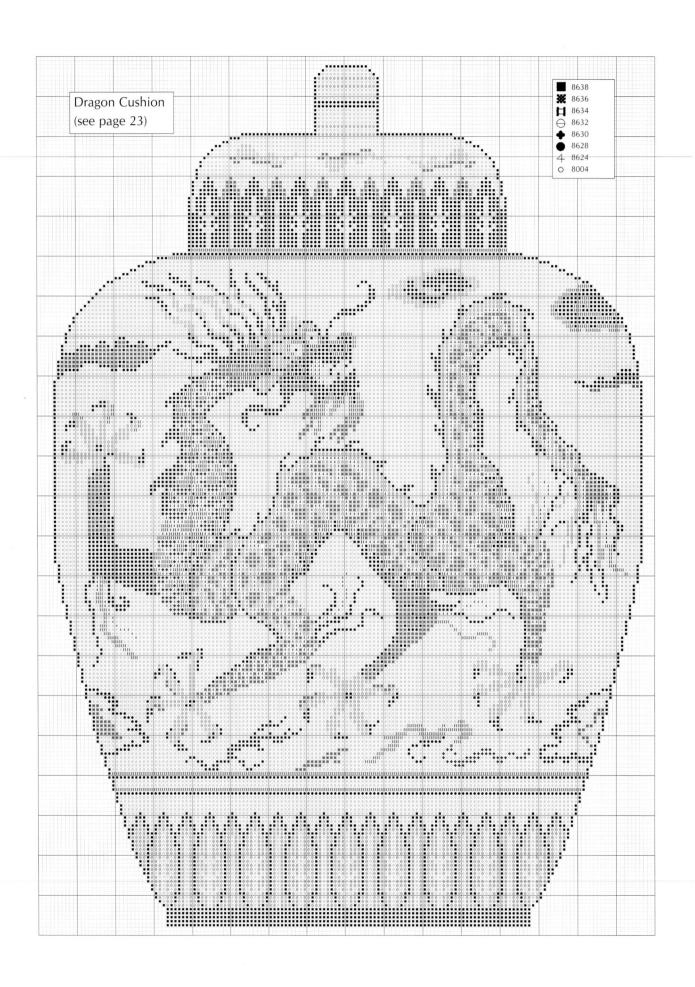

Dragon Cushion
(see page 23)

■	8638
✳	8636
Ⱶ	8634
⊖	8632
◆	8630
●	8628
4	8624
○	8004

Madarin Duck
Cushion
(see page 26)

	8638
	8636
	8634
	8632
	8630
	8628
	8624
	8004

Metallic Flower
Bell-pull
(see page 28)

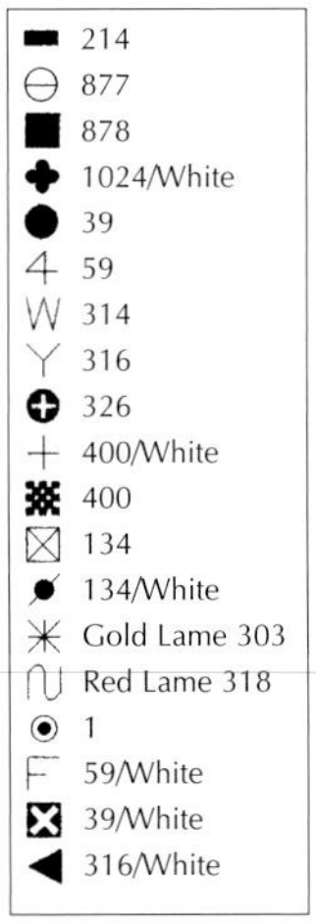

▬	214
⊖	877
■	878
✚	1024/White
●	39
4	59
W	314
Y	316
⊕	326
+	400/White
✳	400
⊠	134
●	134/White
✳	Gold Lame 303
∩	Red Lame 318
⊙	1
F	59/White
☒	39/White
◀	316/White

Metallic Flower
Bell-pull
(see page 28)

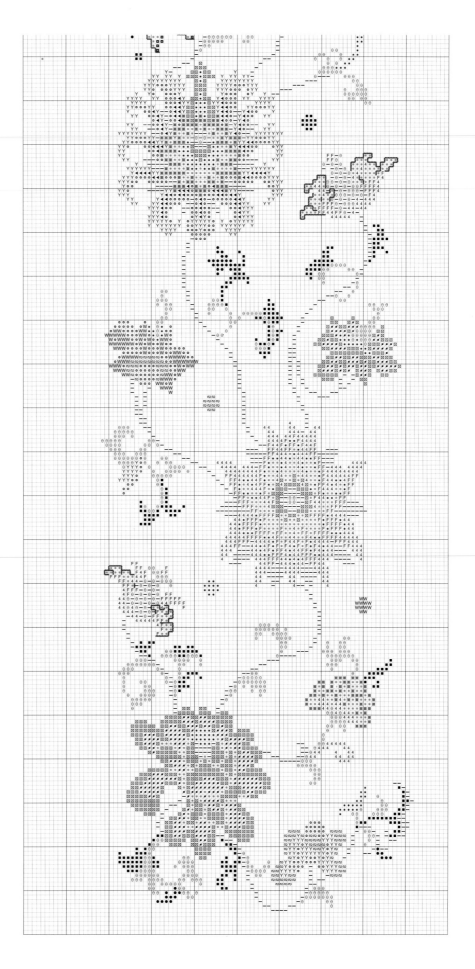

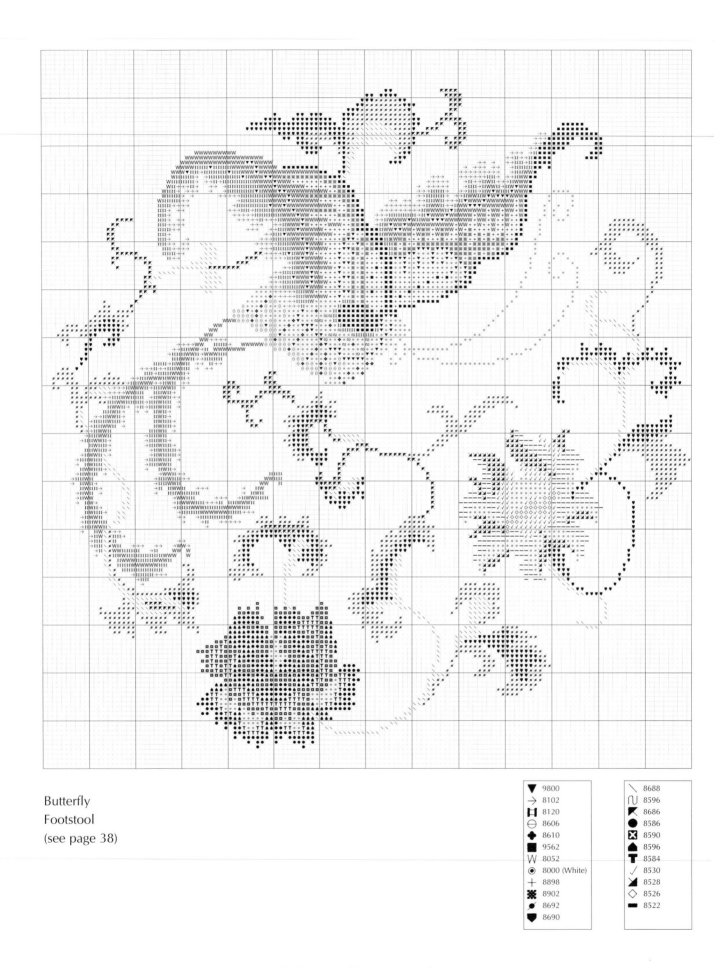

Butterfly
Footstool
(see page 38)

▼ 9800	╲ 8688
→ 8102	∩ 8596
⊟ 8120	◤ 8686
⊖ 8606	● 8586
◆ 8610	⊠ 8590
■ 9562	▲ 8596
W 8052	T 8584
⊙ 8000 (White)	✓ 8530
+ 8898	◢ 8528
✳ 8902	◇ 8526
◗ 8692	▬ 8522
▼ 8690	

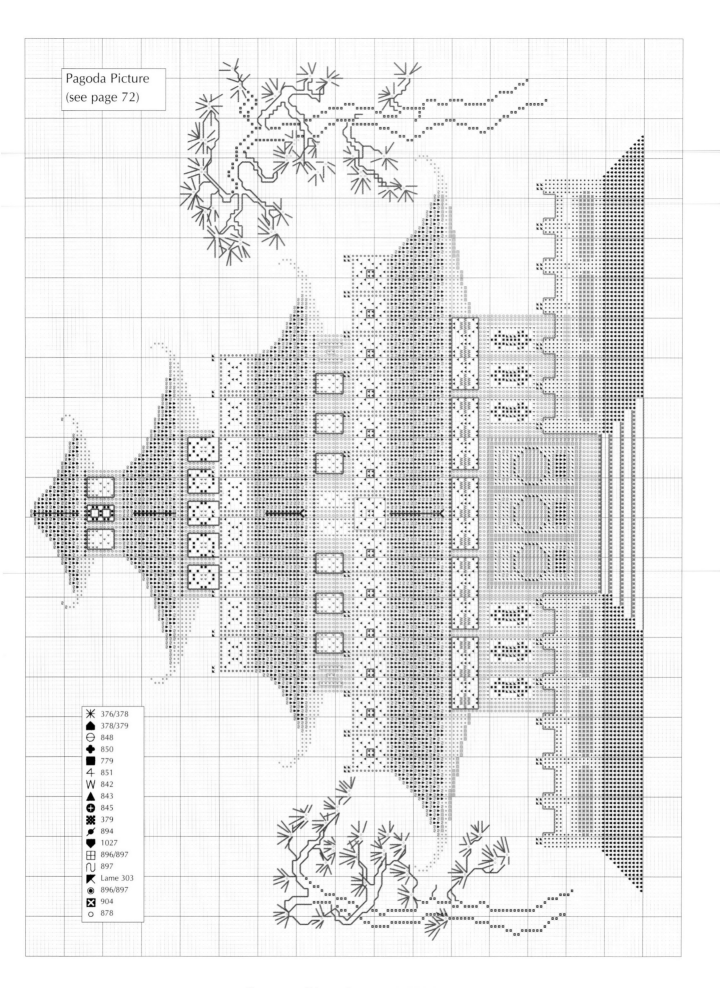

Pagoda Picture
(see page 72)

✳	376/378
⬟	378/379
⊖	848
♣	850
■	779
╄	851
W	842
▲	843
⊕	845
✻	379
✎	894
▼	1027
⊞	896/897
∿	897
⊼	Lame 303
⊙	896/897
⊠	904
○	878

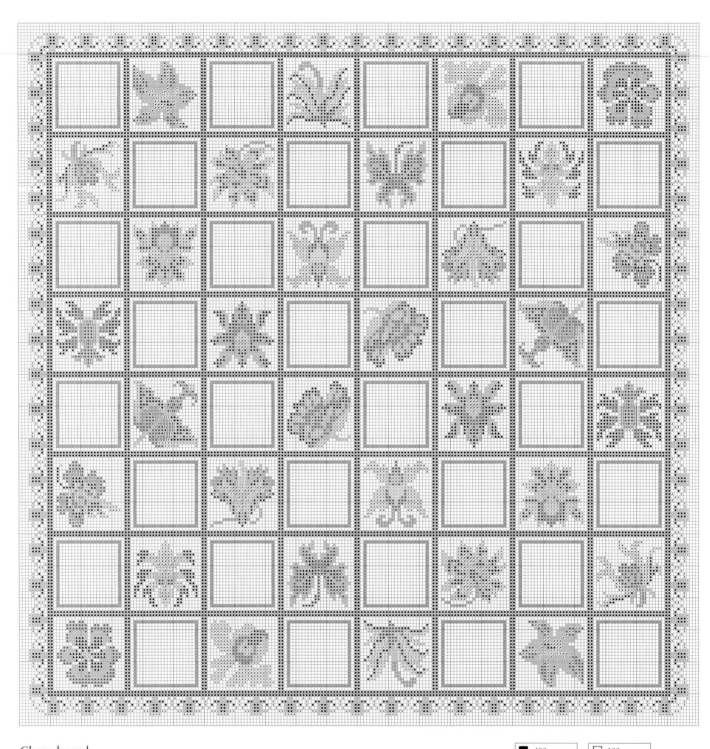

Chess-board
(see page 75)

■ 403	□ 122	
→ 306	▲ 117/Cream	
⊟ 878	⊠ 45	
⊖ 876/878	✳ 45/5975	
✦ 876	✔ 386	
● 337	✳ 337/Cream	
⊿ 5975	⊙ 214	
✛ 117		

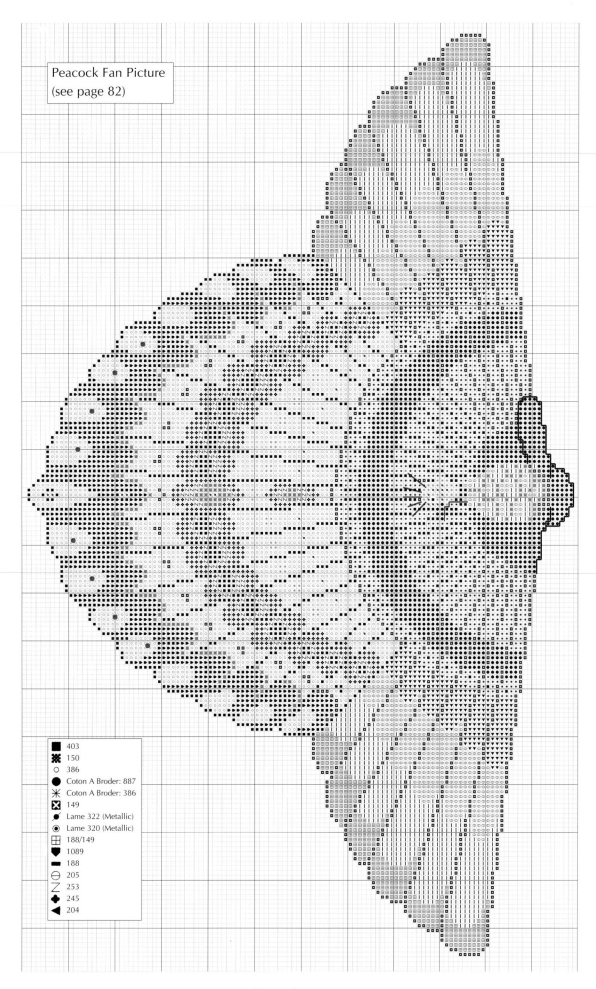

Peacock Fan Picture
(see page 82)

■	403
✳	150
○	386
●	Coton A Broder: 887
✳	Coton A Broder: 386
☒	149
◖	Lame 322 (Metallic)
⊙	Lame 320 (Metallic)
⊞	188/149
▼	1089
▬	188
⊖	205
Z	253
◆	245
◀	204

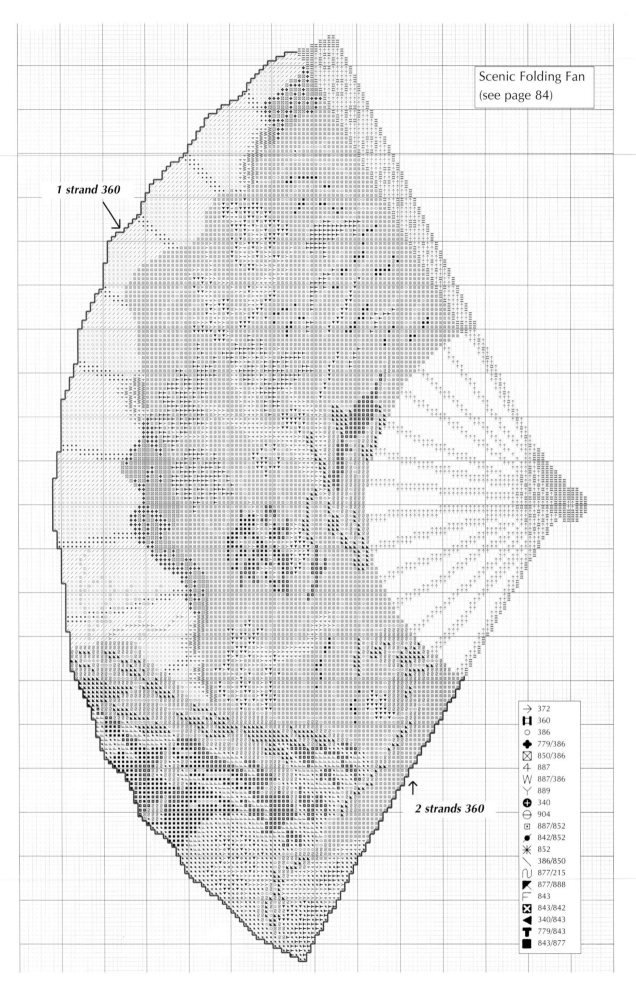

Scenic Folding Fan
(see page 84)

1 strand 360

2 strands 360

→	372
⊞	360
○	386
◆	779/386
⊠	850/386
4	887
W	887/386
Y	889
⊕	340
⊖	904
⊡	887/852
●	842/852
✳	852
\	386/850
∩	877/215
◤	877/888
F	843
⊠	843/842
◀	340/843
T	779/843
■	843/877

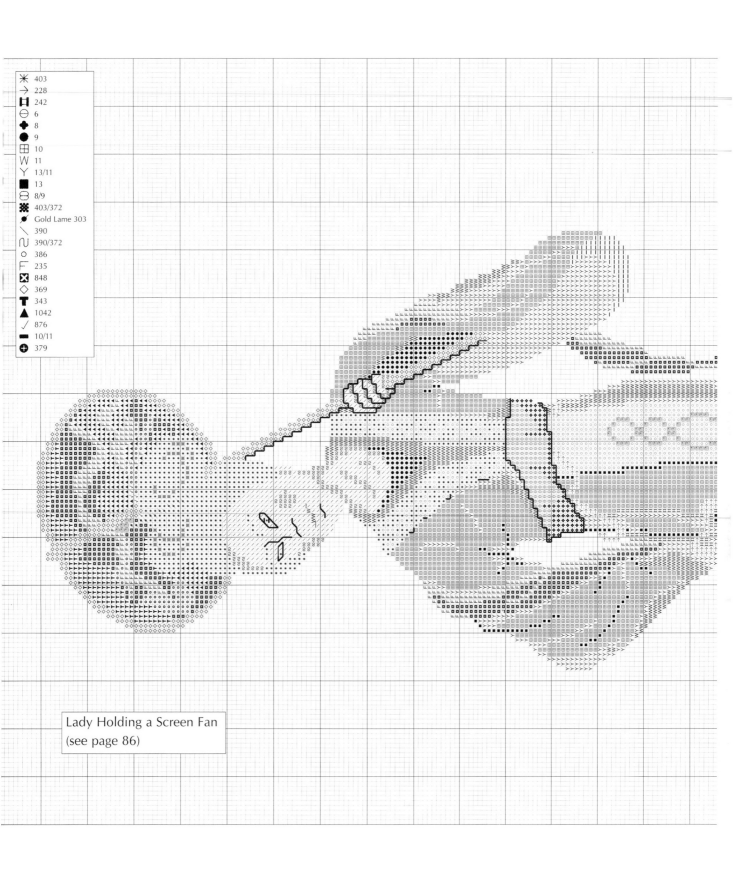

✳	403
→	228
H	242
⊖	6
✚	8
●	9
⊞	10
W	11
Y	13/11
■	13
⊟	8/9
✳	403/372
◗	Gold Lame 303
\	390
∿	390/372
o	386
F	235
☒	848
◇	369
T	343
▲	1042
∕	876
▬	10/11
✛	379

Lady Holding a Screen Fan
(see page 86)

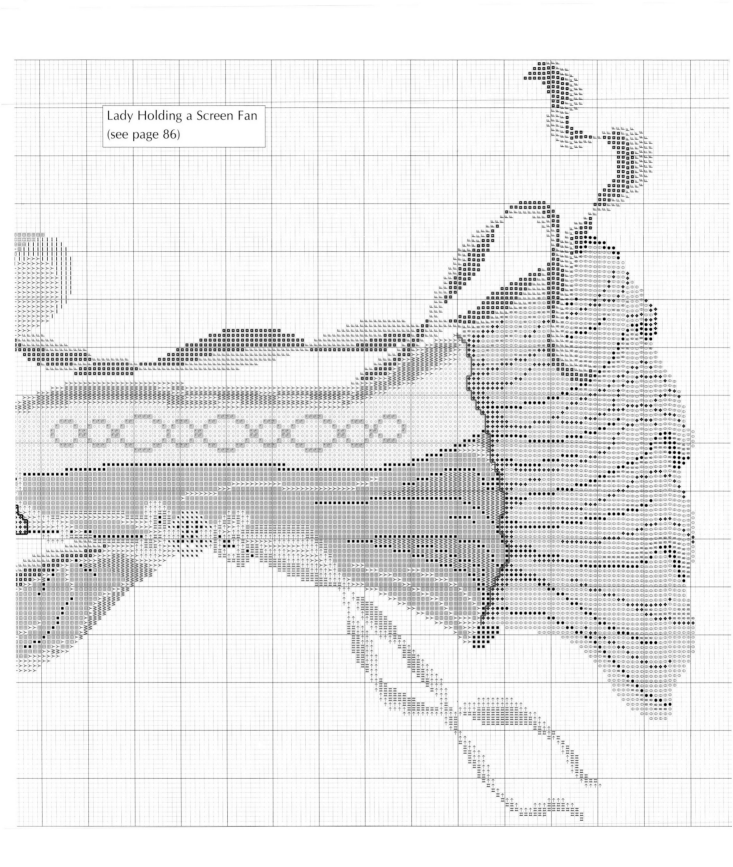

Lady Holding a Screen Fan
(see page 86)

BLACK AND WHITE CHARTS FOR ENLARGING

161

Bird and Flower
Bell-pull, continued
(see page 93)

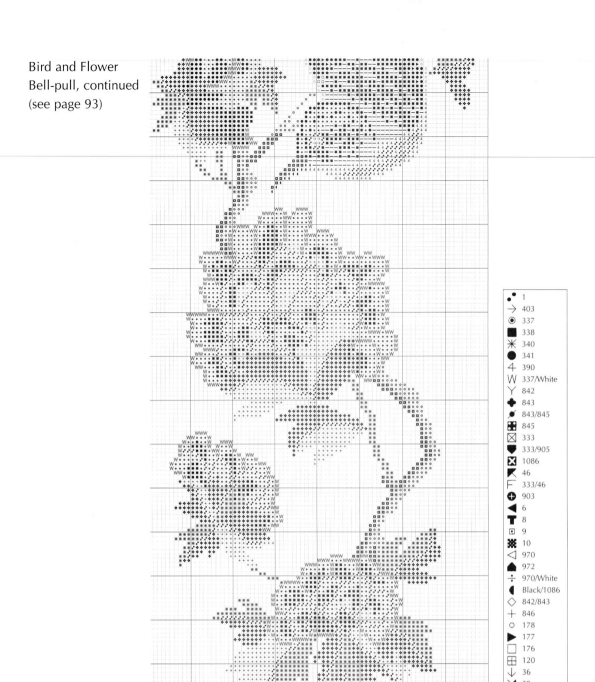

•	1
→	403
⊙	337
■	338
✳	340
●	341
4	390
W	337/White
Y	842
♣	843
✿	843/845
▦	845
⊠	333
♥	333/905
⊠	1086
◤	46
F	333/46
⊕	903
◀	6
T	8
⊡	9
✵	10
◁	970
⬠	972
÷	970/White
◖	Black/1086
◇	842/843
+	846
○	178
►	177
□	176
⊞	120
↓	36
◪	39
♡	36/39
⊖	120/White
△	36/White
▬	338/340
⊤	903/1086

Phoenix Picture
(see page 136) (continues overleaf)

⊠	403
→	341
Ⴂ	339
⊖	338
♣	337
●	337/White
⊹	879
⊞	877
Y	975
⊞	149
✳	132
✎	131
♥	343
\	1096
∽	921
■	390
⊦	390/388
⊠	388
◀	343/388
T	1
⊕	878/149
✳	White/390
▲	1084/390
━	872
○	870
◇	870/White

BLACK AND WHITE CHARTS FOR ENLARGING

Phoenix Picture, continued
(see page 136)

About the Author

Carol was born in Scarborough, North Yorkshire, but has lived in the East Riding of Yorkshire for many years with her husband Alan and two daughters.

She trained as a teacher, and still teaches part-time in her village school. She has always been interested in embroidery and design, and with a friend started a needlework kit business. This has now been sold, and for the last ten years Carol has been a freelance needlework designer, working mainly for magazines and kit companies.

She spends a lot of time walking in the Derbyshire Dales, but some form of embroidery is always at hand. Carol thinks that one of the nicest things about stitching is that it is so portable and can be done almost anywhere.

Carol's first book for Guild of Master Craftsman Publications, *Celtic Cross Stitch Designs*, was published in 1999 and she is currently working on a third book, *Making Miniature Chinese Rugs and Carpets*, for publication in 2002.

MAGAZINES

WOODTURNING ✦ WOODCARVING ✦ FURNITURE & CABINETMAKING
THE ROUTER ✦ WOODWORKING
THE DOLLS' HOUSE MAGAZINE ✦ WATER GARDENING
OUTDOOR PHOTOGRAPHY ✦ BLACK & WHITE PHOTOGRAPHY
BUSINESSMATTERS

The above represents a full list of all titles currently published or scheduled to be published.
All are available direct from the Publishers or through bookshops, newsagents and specialist retailers.
To place an order, or to obtain a complete catalogue, contact:

GMC Publications,
Castle Place, 166 High Street, Lewes, East Sussex BN7 1XU, United Kingdom
Tel: 01273 488005 Fax: 01273 478606
E-mail: pubs@thegmcgroup.com

Orders by credit card are accepted